D0323895

UNTIMELY DEMISE

A DARKLY HUMOROUS PRESENTATION OF 365 DEADLY DEEDS

WILLIAM DYLAN POWELL

ILLUSTRATED BY ALEX KALOMERIS

CIDER MILL PRESS

BOOK PUBLISHERS

KENNEBUNKPORT, ME

THIS IS A WORK OF HUMOR AND IS MEANT TO BE TAKEN AS SUCH. THIS BOOK BY NO MEANS CONDONES MURDER OR VIOLENCE OF ANY KIND.

Books published by Cider Mill Press Book Publishers are available at special discounts for bulk purchases in the United States by corporations, institutions, and other organizations. For more information, please contact the publisher.

Cider Mill Press Book Publishers
"Where good books are ready for press"
PO Box 454, 12 Spring Street, Kennebunkport, Maine 04046

Visit us on the Web! www.cidermillpress.com

Illustrations by Alex Kalomeris
Cover design by Anna Ruth Taylor
Interior design by Sara Corbett

Printed in the United States

1 2 3 4 5 6 7 8 9 0

First Edition

U ntimely Demise: *365 Ways to Off Someone* is a daily reminder of some of the hundreds of ways humans have devised to kill. People can be mundanely narrow-minded in their everyday lives, but when it comes to murder, their creativity seems to know no bounds. Meant to be consumed in small sips, like the poisoned tea in an Agatha Christie novel, our dark journey will take us to a different killer corner—one per day for a year—of the murderous mind, as well as the deadly details in these savage acts.

For instance:

KILLER MOVES explores deadly martial arts techniques from fighting arts, such as kung fu, karate, ninjutsu, and more.

PERNICIOUS POISONS serves up examples of poisons, venoms, and other deadly substances and situations involving toxic foul play.

MURDER MOST STRANGE showcases some of the most bizarre murder methods known to mankind.

THUG LIFE gives examples of killing from the criminal class, from old school Italian Mafiosos to the gangsters of today.

FATAL FIREARMS spotlights all kinds of guns from around the world, giving an overview of their history, use and misuse, technical capabilities, and more.

SLASHER MADNESS presents cutting edge examples of the world's most murderous knives, swords, and other bladed weapons.

SNEAKY SABOTAGE gives examples of murder made to look accidental—from roadways to stairways, one can never be too careful!

Humankind has long been driven to explore the grim experiences and possibilities of the criminal mind, but as you gaze into the abyss of murder that follows, bear in mind that while the topic is merely entertainment today, one never knows about tomorrow…

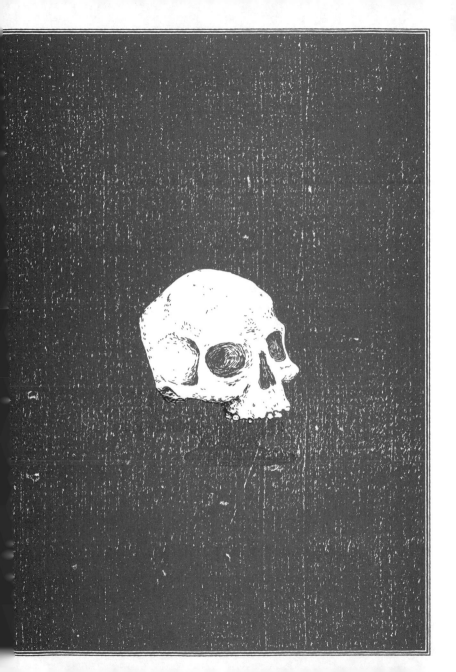

APPLIANCE IN BATHTUB

The bathtub is a place to relax and soak away your stress…
unless you add a plugged-in toaster. Then it's just plain murder
by electrocution. In Hollywood, sparks fly left and right from
a cinematic hailstorm of hair dryers, curling irons, toasters, and other
appliances chucked into baths. In real life, such occurrences are much
more rare, but just as deadly. While there's no guarantee that throwing
an appliance into a tub will always do the trick—since the type of
appliance, where it falls in relation to the tub's metal components, the
size of the appliance's heating element, and the actual composition
of the water all play a factor—tossing an appliance with any kind of
heating element that has direct electricity-to-water contact is pretty
likely to ruin someone's day. Or at least ruin their toast.

OKINAWAN SAI

A *sai* is a traditional Okinawan three-pronged martial arts
weapon composed of a long prong with a handle on one
end—like a heavy iron skewer—and a sharp two-pronged
hilt. They are traditionally used in pairs, one in each hand. Some say
these intimidating weapons were originally used as farm implements,
to plant rice or bale hay. Others say they were developed by the
Okinawan police in the 1600s. Whatever their origin, *sai* can be
used defensively, as a blunt force weapon, or to poke victims as one

pokes a toothpick into a finger sandwich. The prongs can block and trap an opponent's weapon, and the grip allows the fighter to flick them around back and forth in either "smack" or "skewer" mode. Not to mention, the sai also looks like it could be used to make some killer kabobs in the kitchen.

- - - - - - - - - - **PERNICIOUS POISONS** - - - - - - - - - -

DEADLY NIGHTSHADE
(ATROPA BELLADONNA)

Deadly Nightshade is a particularly poisonous plant in the *Solanaceae* family, with highly toxic roots, green leaves, purple flowers, and black berries. The plant's genus name "Atropa" comes from Atropos (the Greek goddess of Fate responsible for severing the thread of life); and "belladonna," meaning "beautiful woman" in Italian, likely derived from the plant's one-time cosmetic use to dilate pupils. Nightshade is rich in tropane alkaloids, notably atropine; when consumed, chemicals in the plant disable the neurotransmitter acetylcholine. The result is imbalance, slurred speech, delirium, paralysis, and many other not-super-fun symptoms. Nightshade is especially dangerous to have around children and animals, since its berries are pretty and sweet, and experts estimate it takes only three to five to kill a small child—good reason to be able to identify this toxic plant and make sure it never grows near your house.

TRUE CRIME Roman Emperor Augustus and Roman Emperor Claudius were both rumored to have been poisoned with nightshade.

PIANO WIRE

T hough brass, copper, and iron were all once used in the keyed instruments of the 18th and 19th centuries, today the wires found inside of a piano are made from carbon steel, which is extremely high in tensile strength. Piano wire is thin but strong, made to withstand repeated abuse; so sturdy, it's used for fishing lures, jewelry, industrial cutting, orthodontics and—you guessed it—murder. Killers have used it by looping it around their victims' necks and choking them to death, as seen in films like *From Russia with Love* and *The Godfather*. A real-life satanic cult in Chicago also used piano wire as a part of their deadly repertoire during the early 1980s. Talk about off-key.

TRUE CRIME **A marijuana grower in upstate New York (who may or may not have been suffering from job-induced short-term memory loss) killed himself in the 1990s by driving an ATV into piano wire he himself had set around his farm as a booby trap.**

- - - - - - - - - - PERNICIOUS POISONS - - - - - - - - - -

ARSENIC

A rsenic (symbol: As, atomic number: 33) is a natural element found in the Earth's crust. It has a number of scientific uses, including the manufacturing of semiconductors, wood preservation, pyrotechnics, bronzing, and other industrial applications. Back in Victorian days, arsenic was actually used as a medicinal cure-all. But, of course, it's best known for murder. A number of famous politicians are suspected to have died of arsenic poisoning, including the Chinese Emperor Guangxu, Bolivian President Simon Bolivar, and Iraq's King Faisal. Consuming arsenic keeps the body from using thiamine, an essential vitamin. The result? Symptoms from stomach pain to hair loss to night blindness—and eventually, death.

DEADLY DETAILS **While arsenic is infamous for its murderous legacy, arsenic poisoning most commonly occurs from ground water. Shrimp actually contain a type of arsenic called arsenobetaine, but it's not harmful to humans.**

- - - - - - - - - - - SLASHER MADNESS - - - - - - - - - - - -

BALISONG KNIFE

B alisongs were made popular in the 1970s and 1980s, when every bad martial arts movie sported a thug flipping around these flashy blades. These murder-worthy weapons are foldable pocket knives with two rotating handles meant to open and close quickly, requiring only one hand. Also commonly known as a "butterfly knife" (because when used by a skilled practitioner, the blades' motion resembles the beautiful fluttering wings of a butterfly … that can kill you), the flashy tricks and flipping open of the knife does make it an intimidating weapon. Many countries and states have now outlawed the Balisong because so many unskilled operators of the weapon hurt *themselves* while using it. Ouch!

DEADLY DETAILS **Traditionally, the Balisong knife was used by the Filipino people, especially in the Tagalog region, and they're sometimes known as Batangas knives after the province of that same name in the Philippines.**

WING CHUN CHAIN PUNCH

Wing Chun (which translates as "forever spring"—not to be confused with the 1980s British band Wang Chun, which means "yellow bell" in Chinese) is a Chinese martial art made popular by Bruce Lee (and more recently, the *Ip Man* films, semi-biographical accounts of Lee's martial art master). The art has its roots in the Shaolin temple, and was supposedly created by a Buddhist nun. Wing Chun's strategy is to dominate the opponent's centerline with vicious punches. One of its core techniques is called the chain punch—a continual series of rapid punches to the opponent's chest. It's possible for an expert in Wing Chun to actually cause fatal heart failure in an opponent using this technique, making for one murderous beat-down.

KARATE KNIFE-HAND

Knife Hand is a common technique in many martial arts, especially Japanese Karate and Korean Taekwondo, and is what many non-martial artists call a "karate chop." In this strike, the fighter points his or her elbow at the target, extends his arm, then strikes the victim with the edge of his hand. The striker uses a strong stance or footwork and the power of hip rotation to put his or her whole body into the blow. It's a powerful strike. Someone good at this can use the knife-hand to strike the carotid artery, causing the artery to constrict and deny the brain proper blood flow. With such a precise strike, loss of consciousness would occur—and human bodies being inherently fragile, death is absolutely possible, especially if the victim hits the pavement.

POP CULTURE In your average James Bond movie, bad guys are put to sleep left and right using the knife-hand strike. In real life, if Daniel Craig or Sean Connery actually knife-handed someone, the victim's reaction would probably be: "Ouch! Hey, great suit."

- - - - - - - - - **MURDER MOST STRANGE** - - - - - - - - -

GUILLOTINE

ive la Revolution! Most people know guillotines for their iconic role during the French Revolution. They consist of a tall wooden frame, from which a weighted and angled blade is suspended. The victim is placed below the blade, and decapitated when the heavy blade is released. Guillotines were sort of the electric chair of old, popularly used to behead the legally condemned—though often with some concern over how quickly those being executed were relieved of their suffering. Tales of detached heads blinking, frowning, or otherwise expressing themselves haunted the nightmares of those witnessing execution by this cruel decree.

DEADLY DETAILS A guillotine has been the undoing of many a man and woman throughout the ages—by some estimates, as many as 15,000 people were executed via guillotine during the French Revolution alone, and France continued to use the guillotine in an official capacity up until 1977!

JAPANESE SAMURAI SWORD

The sword of the Samurai, or *katana*, has been one of the most efficient and elegant murder weapons known to man. A long sword gripped with two hands, it features a curved single-edge blade and a distinctive circular guard with a wrapped grip. The *katana* as we know it dates back to about 8th century Japan. What makes a traditional *katana* such a fearsome weapon, aside from the Samurai's extensive training, is its tremendous strength and sharpness. This is achieved by a distinctive forging process that involves folding the metal several times to achieve what many experts call the finest swords created by mankind. Most modern *katanas* made today aren't made in this traditional manner—but could still off someone.

DAGGER

A dagger is perhaps the first known variety of knife, dating back to Neolithic times (around 10,000 BC), and a means of personal defense for the common man. Early daggers were primitive affairs carved from flint or animal bones, with straight, double-edged blades used for either stabbing or slashing. Refinements and materials evolved over the centuries, but the general shape and deadliness of this basic weapon has not much changed since the dawn of man's most basic technologies. Today, they are largely the purview of military close-combat applications and specialty collectors—often symbolic in nature. But they're still capable of everyday murder.

ARSON

Many arsonists (people who intentionally set fire to a building, land, or vehicle) commit their crimes to collect insurance money, to cover up another crime, for the thrill they get—or, of course, to commit murder. Most use an accelerant such as gasoline. There have been a number of famous arsonists throughout history, and some modern-day arsonists have caused thousands of fires before being apprehended. One of the most recent notables was David Berkowitz, or the "Son of Sam." Most people know him as the notorious serial killer who terrorized the streets of New York in the 1970s, but he was also a compulsive arsonist. It was an act of arson committed against a neighbor that eventually led to his arrest. The good news? Arsonists often can't stop and eventually get burned by the long arm of the law.

BRASS KNUCKLES

Y ou can totally murder somebody with brass knuckles or "knuckle dusters." While over the years they've been made of wood, cast iron, brass, lead, chrome, and composite, these weapons are now usually composed of a single piece of steel or brass, made to fit around the knuckles of each finger to enhance the impact of a punch. Weapons of this nature date to a number of cultures and ages but they didn't pop up in the United States until the 1800s. They were often employed by soldiers in the Civil War, and sometimes even attached to knives in WWI and WWII to aid in trench warfare. Their killer potential is typically realized by applying blunt force trauma to the head of the victim, causing a fracturing of the skull or brain hemorrhage. It's also possible to cause heart failure or a ruptured spleen with hard strikes using brass knuckles.

STRAIGHT RAZOR

B ack before "safety razors" (i.e. what people buy in the store today), the straight razor—a flat, straight blade that folds into a long handle like a pocketknife—was how well-groomed folks stayed smooth. One would foam up the skin with a brush and soap, finely sharpen the razor on a "strop" (basically a strip of leather), and then use the super-sharp razor for a nice, close shave…and sometimes more. First made in England back in the 1600s, these razors were also old-school murder weapons, popular for their concealability and efficiency. Many a man and woman used this useful tool for nefarious purposes, and many an old school shaver has given them up after seeing *Sweeney Todd*.

CAR BRAKES

A popular method of murder in the movies: the good guy gets his flashy car up to speed and then panics when the brake pedal falls uselessly to the floor. This is an especially cold-blooded way to kill since it also puts innocent bystanders on the road at risk. In 2012, a UK man was arrested for cutting the brake lines in his girlfriend's car after an argument (the lucky lady survived). But while older cars had just one set of brake lines (so that if the line was cut badly or a pinhole leak bled the system, the vehicle had no brakes at all), thankfully, modern vehicles have more robust braking systems, with a master cylinder that controls independent front and rear brake systems—so if one set goes out, you still have the other. On the other hand, these days, brake-tampering potential has even gone high-tech. Researchers at a recent tech conference found a way to electronically "cut the brake line" of a Corvette by hacking into the software that manages a vehicle's actual hardware!

THAI ROUND KICK

P ractitioners of Muay Thai, or Thai Kickboxing, are some of the fiercest, most well-conditioned fighters on the planet— utilizing their fists, feet, elbows, knees, and a number of specialized techniques. To execute a potentially lethal Thai roundhouse kick, fighters pivot on the ball of their forward foot, then swing their hips, putting their whole bodies behind the motion, and let the other foot whip around like a baseball bat. The effect is devastating—and not just because of the sheer power involved. When normal folks hit their shin on a coffee table it hurts like crazy, but traditional Thai fighters condition their shinbones through specific training and ointments until they are hard as hammers. The result is that a solid Thai roundhouse kick to the head not only knocks people out, but could also cause a fatal brain bleed.

- - - - - - - - - - - **PERNICIOUS POISONS** - - - - - - - - - - -
CYANIDE

C yanide is a chemical compound composed of carbon and a triple-bonded nitrogen atom. There is more than one type of cyanide, and many are found in nature (such as in apricot pits and apple seeds). Burning synthetic materials such as polyurethane or vinyl also creates cyanide—which is one reason why the smoke from burning buildings can be so toxic. Some cyanides are even found in outer space! But find the wrong type in your cup of coffee, and you've also found murder. When ingested, cyanide renders the body unable to use oxygen. And your body really needs oxygen—especially the heart, brain, and lungs. Some say cyanide smells like bitter almonds, but not always. Still, best be on the alert if your coffee tastes funny.

TRUE CRIME In 1978, 912 members of a cult called "The People's Temple" died from drinking Kool-Aid laced with cyanide, after their leader ordered his followers to drink the toxic concoction. Hence the phrase, "don't drink the Kool-Aid."

MANDRAKE

Another member of the nightshade family, *Mandrake officinarum* is a green leafy plant with thick, robust roots resembling a turnip. And it totally tastes like murder. Also known as Satan's Apple, almost all of this plant is poisonous—containing high levels of scopolamine, hyoscyamine, and atropine, just like Belladonna. All of these are toxic alkaloids that mess with your head, and cause symptoms like vomiting and asphyxiation. Back in the day, practitioners of witchcraft included mandrake in much of their mystical jiggery-pokery. Legend has it that not only does mandrake look super-creepy and vaguely humanoid, but that the plant screams when pulled from the ground, killing everyone within earshot. It does, however, have some anesthetic medicinal applications… assuming the magic death scream doesn't kill you first.

CATTLE STAMPEDE

A stampede is a collective running of herd animals when they've been spooked. If you haven't spent much time on a ranch, cows are heavy. Really heavy. Your average American cow weighs around 1,350 pounds (about 590 kilos). That's about two-fifths of the weight of an average passenger car. So getting caught in a cattle stampede is like stepping out into traffic during rush hour! Even in today's modern world, an estimated twenty people a year die via stampede. (And that doesn't include shopping stampedes on Black Friday.) So here's hoping that you never encounter anyone with evil intentions who happens to have a bunch of spare cattle and a designation as beneficiary on your life insurance policy.

- - - - - - - - - MURDER MOST STRANGE - - - - - - - - -

FORKS

F orks have traditionally been popular murder weapons inside the prison system—with prisoners stealing them from the cafeteria and then sharpening them to a deadly edge for use against enemies. But there are examples from outside the big house as well. For instance, in 2013, a Mississippi man murdered a friend by stabbing him in the heart with a fork; that same year, a student at the University of Texas was stabbed with a fork by a former boyfriend, who'd followed her all the way from China just to stab her in the nose (the victim survived the attack). Guess it wasn't her *tine* to die.

- - - - - - - - - - - - - THUG LIFE - - - - - - - - - - - - -

SAP

A sap, also known as a blackjack, is a flat piece of elongated leather shaped rather like a beaver's tail (though much smaller) and filled with heavy lead shot or similar substances. Being hit with a sap can cause lacerations, fractured bones, or death. This simple, small, and easily concealable mini-club could be used to murder somebody no problem—but fortunately it's usually only used by police officers to help keep the streets safe. Police also use "sap gloves" which have the same hard striking surfaces actually sewn into the knuckles or palms of the glove. So pay your freakin' parking tickets.

These weapons are called saps because back in the day, some were actually filled with tree sap.

- - - - - - - - - - - SLASHER MADNESS - - - - - - - - - - -

SWITCHBLADE

A switchblade knife opens automatically using mechanical force. There are a number of different variations, but most open at the touch of a button and are then manually pushed closed against a locking mechanism. When most people envision a switchblade, they picture what's known as an Italian stiletto—black handled with silver trim and a bayonet-style blade. As a tactical fighting or utilitarian knife, the switchblade isn't very practical, but it does have a warranted intimidation factor. The knife has gained a reputation over the years as the conventional tool of gangsters, criminals, and wayward youth. And, of course, killers.

POP CULTURE The stiletto switchblade used by James Dean in *Rebel Without a Cause* was recently auctioned for $12,000!

- - - - - - - - MURDER MOST STRANGE - - - - - - - -

ENTOMBING
or BURYING ALIVE

Entombment means to build or bury a structure in such a way as to trap a victim inside, or to enclose an unfortunate soul into the foundation of a building or within a wall, as in

Edgar Allan Poe's classic "The Cask of Amontillado" or Linda Fairstein's novel *Entombed*. Scary! It can also mean smothering someone entirely in a substance like concrete, which hardens around the victim. In ancient times many societies used live burial as a method of capital punishment for certain crimes, and especially brutal modern regimes such as the Nazis, Cambodia's Khmer Rouge, and Mao Tse Tung's Communist party have also used premature burial as a form of execution.

DEADLY DETAILS The technical name for being buried alive is "vivisepulture."

------------- **KILLER MOVES** --------------

FILIPINO STICK ATTACK

The Filipino martial art of Kali (also called Arnis or Eskrima) is known for its devastatingly effective weapon attacks, including deadly short stick fighting techniques. Practitioners learn to "flow" with the sticks, one move seamlessly flowing into the other, like a hurricane of pain. A pair of these sticks—typically made of rattan, which is light and hard and super-painful when you're on the receiving end—gives an experienced fighter range and a variety of defensive and offensive techniques. Traditional hardwood versions of the weapons are even more deadly.

TRUE CRIME Little known fact: The Portuguese explorer Ferdinand Magellan was killed by natives in the Philippines wielding such weapons during the Battle of Mactan in 1521.

CROSSBOW

crossbow is part bow and arrow, part rifle, and all deadly. Crossbows are composed of a bow mounted on a stock, usually made of wood or composite, and they shoot reusable arrows known as "bolts." The bow is drawn and mechanically locked into place, allowing the shooter to fire the crossbow using a trigger just as one would a conventional rifle. Ancient crossbow bolts have been found dating back to the 5th century BC, and they've been used for murder ever since. Modern crossbows are employed in hunting and fishing, as well as by paramilitary and clandestine forces, due to their relative silence in the field.

GARROTE

A garrote is a brutally simple weapon used to kill someone by choking. They're made from two components—a line of some kind (like a rope, wire, or cable) and a small stick, used to tighten the line around a victim's neck by twisting. The stick is key to the weapon's effectiveness ("garrote" is Spanish for stick), multiplying applied force so there's more pressure than simple strangulation. Murder via garrote dates back to ancient times, but remains common worldwide; the weapon received widespread coverage during the tragic 1996 murder of JonBenét Ramsey.

DEADLY DETAILS **In Medieval times, a device resembling a chair with a garrote hardwired to the back was used as a torture device.**

COLT M-1911

Designed by John Browning, the M-1911 is a semi-automatic handgun that's been the standard to which all other makes are held. The gun runs .45 ACP ammo, holds seven rounds in a detachable magazine and has incredible stopping power (the overall amount of ballistic trauma a gun and its ammunition can deliver). This is all in a design that makes it a reliable killing machine issued to soldiers from World War I all the way up to modern conflicts in Iraq and Afghanistan, and has served as the conventional military service sidearm for much of America's modern history. And while many assume that side arms are issued to help military officers shoot at the enemy, in practice a military officer's sidearm is primarily issued for when those under his or her command won't follow orders. Yikes, better get to peeling those potatoes!

POP CULTURE **Humphrey Bogart sported an M-1911 in the 1942 WWII classic *Casablanca*.**

- - - - - - - - MURDER MOST STRANGE - - - - - - - -

ALCOHOL POISONING

L'chaim! Many folks raise a glass when they want to celebrate life. But it's also certainly possible to kill by forcing someone to drink too much alcohol. Although your body has natural defenses against consuming toxic amounts of liquor—vomiting and passing out are your body's way of saying: "Enough!" Of course, some defenses are stronger than others. Michael "Iron Mike" Malloy, an Irishman living in the Bronx during Prohibition, surely set a record. Some associates tried to kill him in 1933 by giving him unlimited credit at a local speakeasy, hoping to kill him and collect insurance. But after a full day and night of whiskey after whiskey, the man was unfazed. So they poisoned him with methanol. Then antifreeze. Then tacks, ground glass, and metal. Nothing. At the end of the night, they tied him on the bench hoping he'd freeze. Malloy slept through and survived the night (no doubt with a brutal hangover) only to be murdered three months later by the same gang on their TENTH attempt.

TRUE CRIME **In another type of alcohol poisoning altogether, the U.S. government once poisoned industrial alcohol with toxins such as brucine and benzene to scare Americans sober; this effort murdered an estimated 10,000 people!**

HEMLOCK

Hemlock is a green, ferny, sprig-like plant with little white flowers. Scientifically known as *Conium maculatum*, it's actually in the plant family *Apiacaeae* along with several tasty and non-poisonous relatives like carrots and parsley. But you certainly don't want hemlock in your salad. Hemlock contains what are known as piperdine alkaloid toxins, which can cause tremors, stomach aches, coma, and even death (from respiratory failure). Chemically, it's actually pretty similar to nicotine, but so deadly that the ancient Greeks used it as the state's preferred method of execution. Socrates infamously died as a result of hemlock poisoning while a political prisoner in 399 BC.

DEADLY DETAILS The Native Americans also poisoned their arrows with hemlock to improve their odds of victory in combat.

SUFFOCATION AND SMOTHERING

The medical term for the condition caused by suffocation or smothering is "asphyxia," which results in generalized hypoxia—the body's lack of adequate oxygen to keep functioning normally. When you suffocate somebody, you murder them by denying air. This can be done in a number of ways, including covering the victim's nose and mouth with a hand, smothering them with a pillow, or sometimes putting a plastic bag over the victim's head. Two of the most notorious murderers to use this method were Irishmen William Burke and William Hare, who in 1828 suffocated more than a dozen people in Edinburgh, Scotland. Their motive? Selling corpses to a doctor for use in the study of anatomy (suffocation leaves few marks). For the love of science.

- - - - - - - - - - - SLASHER MADNESS - - - - - - - - - - - -

PRISON SHANKS AND SHIVS

A shank or shiv is a homemade knife. Though people use the two terms interchangeably, there is a technical difference between a shank and a shiv: a shank is something that's been filed to a point for the purpose of stabbing (so getting "shanked" means to get stabbed with something that pokes into you); a shiv, on the other hand, is something with an edge that cuts and slashes. Both are popular means of defense (and attack) in prisons around the world, and many people have been murdered by one of these cleverly improvised weapons. In addition to the more obvious materials, like glass and razors, they have also been made from all kinds of unexpected materials, including the spines of books, mattress springs, spoons, toothbrushes, and hairbrushes. Apparently, when it comes to creating deadly weapons within prison, some convicts are pretty darn sharp.

- - - - - - - - - - PERNICIOUS POISONS - - - - - - - - - - -

STRYCHNINE

Most commonly used as rat poison, strychnine is a highly toxic alkaloid crystalline powder found in an Asian evergreen tree called the *Strychnos nux-vomica*. The tree is native to Southeast Asia and Australia, but is known worldwide for its murderous power. Eating or otherwise absorbing strychnine results in one of the most violent toxic reactions known to man: foaming at the mouth, vomiting, muscle convulsions, complete body distortion and abnormal arching, as well as asphyxiation. Alfred Hitchcock, Sir Arthur Conan Doyle, Agatha Christie, and H.G. Wells all used strychnine poisoning in fictional tales of murder, and in real life it's been said that Alexander the Great died of strychnine poisoning—not an especially great way to go.

- - - - - - - - - - - **FATAL FIREARMS** - - - - - - - - - - -

RUGER LCP

The subcompact Ruger LCP semi-automatic .380-caliber handgun was made as a concealed firearm to help citizens protect themselves against criminals. With a six-shot magazine plus an additional round in the chamber, the Arizona-made LCP packs a deadly punch. These reliable little pistols have flooded the streets since production began in 2008. Sometimes powerful things come in small packages—even when it comes to murder.

TRUE STORIES **Former Texas Governor Rick Perry brought attention to this gun in 2010, when he used one while out jogging to shoot a coyote that was attacking his daughter's Labrador retriever.**

- - - - - - - - - - - **SNEAKY SABOTAGE** - - - - - - - - - - -

EVIL NURSE

Nursing staff are critical to delivering quality medical care, and they often know more about what's happening on the patient front lines than the doctors they're supporting. But when these medical professionals become unstable, they can be equally good at murder. From improper dosing to tampering with equipment or outright poisoning, evil nurses who prey on people at their most vulnerable are some of the creepiest killers around. Distressingly, since such crimes can be hard to detect, many times these disturbed individuals drift from hospital to hospital, leaving on suspicious terms. Best not to get sick.

TRUE CRIME **One of the most notorious killer nurse cases in modern history were the Lainz Angels of Death—four nurses in 1980s Vienna, Austria, who were together convicted of killing dozens of patients (and suspected of killing as many as 200!).**

- - - - - - - - - - - **FATAL FIREARMS** - - - - - - - - - - -

AK-47

The AK-47 is arguably the world's most famous firearm, both for its military service and its deadliness. Officially known as the *Avtomat Kalashnikova*, the AK-47 is a Russian-designed, selective-fire rifle originally used by the Soviet military in 1949. One of the modern world's first mass-produced, reliable machine guns, it fires 7.62x39mm rounds and became one of the most popular guns in the world. Simple, affordable, and durable—using and stripping the AK-47 can be taught in under an hour. Unfortunately, it's not always responsible citizens who are doing the learning. Its ease of use and reliable firepower have also made the AK-47 popular with gang members, drug cartels, terrorists, mass murderers, and warlords. You'll see these guns in practically every movie featuring Soviet-era soldiers, including the original *Red Dawn* from 1984. Wolverines!

B*ATTLE* *A*XE

A battle axe is a heavy axe that, as the name implies, was specifically designed to kill. Made for either two hands or one, they could be hurled or swung. The blade was often crescent-shaped, and when not used for fighting, they were practical tools. Popular during the Middle Ages from the fifth to the fifteen centuries, and vastly improved upon during the Bronze Age, most cultures made use of them as martial weapons in one form or another.

TRUE CRIME In 2010, the teenage nephew of a serial killer murdered a friend with a Medieval-style battle axe—in the same Australian state forest where at least seven of his uncle's victims were found buried in the 1990s. And those aren't even the only bodies that have been found in that now infamous murder forest. If people still go there, that must be one beautiful park!

HEROIN

You can easily kill someone, including yourself, with heroin. Heroin is an opioid analgesic that's derived from morphine (made from the opium poppy plant). Classified as a depressant, heroin is a powdery or tar-like substance that can be smoked, injected or snorted. The user gets a feeling of euphoria, as well as a boatload of harmful side effects, both immediate and long-term. Murder by heroin often occurs by giving the victim a fatal dose, whether by tainting the drugs or providing a drug with extreme potency. The FBI reported that Las Vegas gaming mogul Ted Binion was at one time the target of a heroin overdose assassination plot by Vegas mob bosses as an attempt at power consolidation (Binion died shortly thereafter, his initial accused murderers having been acquitted). Heroin is highly addictive, and simply giving an addict access to the drug can be absolutely murderous.

DEADLY DETAILS The long-term, deadly health effects of heroin are well-documented. Even stopping use can cause severe withdrawal, which can in turn be fatal as well.

- - - - - - - - - - - FATAL FIREARMS - - - - - - - - - - -

WALTHER PPK

Today only sold in .380-caliber, the Walther PPK is a semi-automatic handgun that holds 6-7 rounds and has a short, 3.3-inch barrel. The PPK stands for *Polizei Pistolen Krimminal*, or Criminal/Police Pistol. Popular as a concealed firearm, this German-made gun packs a murderously powerful punch.

The Walther PPK is the firearm famously carried by international super-spy James Bond. Though the fictional Ian Fleming character used many weapons across the generations of stories and movies, this 7.65mm handgun was originally introduced to the character in *Dr. No*. Since then, it has become a symbol of international espionage and intrigue.

TRUE CRIME **Lesser known: Hitler used a Walther PPK when committing suicide.**

- - - - - - - - - - - - SNEAKY SABOTAGE - - - - - - - - - - - -

FRIENDLY FIRE

L ike General Sherman said, "War is Hell." Unintentionally shooting, blowing up, or otherwise causing the death of a soldier who's on your side is a tragic and seemingly unavoidable phenomenon. Except it's not always an accident. Incidents of murdering a fellow soldier in the field date back to some of the earliest recorded battles—especially once the use of firearms and explosives became commonplace. In U.S. military circles, "fragging" was a common term to describe such a murder (named after the Vietnam-era fragmentation grenade that could be thrown at an unaware recipient and blamed on the enemy), most often of a commanding officer unpopular with his troops. But while there were hundreds of "fragging" incidents during the Vietnam War, there were only two such official incidents among U.S. forces in Iraq and Afghanistan. This is possibly due to the U.S. no longer using the draft; either that, or modern battlefield communications means that today, such crimes could wind up on YouTube before the participants got back to base.

THROWN FROM HEIGHTS

T hrowing someone off of a cliff, building, or other high place has been a tried and true method of murder since biblical times, when James, Jesus' half-brother, was supposedly hurled from the summit of a temple in 62 AD. And in today's multi-story industrial prison complexes, sending somebody over the rail is a murderously common way to dispatch prison rivals. All it takes is a little momentum, and a lot of crazy. Especially in the movies: in the 1956 film noir *A Kiss Before Dying*, a young and crazed Robert Wagner throws his wealthy and pregnant fiancé off a building and then hopes to marry her sister. In the 2006 Martin Scorsese gangster film *The Departed*, Martin Sheen's character also takes the big fall. No wonder so many people are scared of heights!

- - - - - - - - - MURDER MOST STRANGE - - - - - - - - -

GENETICALLY ENGINEERED *BIOWEAPONS*

T alk about super-scary murder stuff! Bioweapons refer to the use of biological or infectious entities such as viruses to kill or otherwise harm people. They come in a variety of terrifying bacteria and toxins ranging from smallpox to the plague. Even insects—that's right, bugs—can be used to attack people or crops. But custom-engineered bioweapons are especially creepy: designed to only infect specific types of people at the DNA level. Because of advances in genome sequencing, scientists may soon be able to create Orwellian nightmare weapons that kill people of a certain genetic makeup (such as, for example, those predisposed to like Justin Bieber's music. What kind of quality of life do those poor folks have anyway?).

- - - - - - - - - - - - - **KILLER MOVES** - - - - - - - - - - - - -

JIU JITSU CHOKE HOLD

J iu Jitsu is a traditional martial art that specializes in throws, holds, grappling, and joint locks. Many people have taken up this martial art in recent years with the rise in popularity of Mixed Martial Arts (MMA) sport fighting. A Jiu Jitsu practitioner could easily murder someone with one of the art's deadly chokeholds— which use leverage to restrict the flow of air or blood to the victim's brain. This can be done either by restricting the carotid arteries or jugular, in the case of a "sleeper" choke or by causing asphyxia via a compression of the airway. Hold either type of chokehold long enough, and you'll also be holding onto a murder rap.

TRUE CRIME **In 2012, a 24-year-old Louisiana man accidentally choked his cousin to death using a rear naked choke, a type of choke hold applied from behind, not realizing the lethality of the technique.**

- - - - - - - - - - - - - **THUG LIFE** - - - - - - - - - - - - -

HOMEMADE BOMB

H omemade bombs are relatively easy to make, yet can inflict terrible damage on people and property. Two of the most common types are letter bombs and car bombs. Letter bombs look like regular old pieces of mail—but explode when opened, firing deadly debris at anyone nearby. Car bombs tend to explode either when a car door is opened, a car alarm is disarmed (using the remote control frequency), or the car's ignition is started. The mafia is suspected of using car bombs to this day, especially in Italy (though it's hard to tell, because Italian-made cars tend to blow up on their own anyway), and convicted murderer, Harvard grad, and all-around crazy person Ted Kaczynski acknowledged responsibility for sixteen homemade bomb attacks over a period of twenty years.

DEADLY DETAILS **Super-secure facilities often use a mirror on the end of a long pole to look for explosives mounted under a vehicle.**

- - - - - - - - - - - FATAL FIREARMS - - - - - - - - - - -

UZI

An Uzi is a specific brand of Israeli submachine gun. Short and compact, the weapon was designed by Major Uziel Gal (hence the name) and introduced in the 1950s. It quickly became common within the Israeli Defense Forces and was soon exported to military, security, and law enforcement groups around the world. The original Uzi fired a 9mm caliber, and came with a 25-round magazine. Wildly popular around the world from Europe to Asia, even the U.S. Secret Service used them as their submachine gun of choice until the '90s, when they switched to the more upscale Heckler & Koch M5. The Uzi's compact size makes it dangerously concealable, and perfect for murder.

- - - - - - - - - - - SLASHER MADNESS - - - - - - - - - - -

HATCHET

A hatchet is a small axe with a short handle and single blade that's designed for use with one hand. A hatchet is one of Man's earliest known hand tools—dating back easily to 6,000 BC—

and while typically used to chop wood, could positively be used for murder. Hatchets and axes were once used in battle, and even today are standard issue for certain military units (though more for their utilitarian, and not martial, value). Regardless, a hatchet is still a deadly weapon. The most infamous instance of murder using a hatchet was in 1892, when Massachusetts resident Lizzie Borden was charged with the murder of her father and stepmother. Borden was actually acquitted of the crime, yet hung around her hometown for the rest of her life despite the whispers and gossip. Nobody else was ever charged with her parents' murders.

DEADLY DETAILS The word "hatchet" is derived from the French word "hachette" or "hache," which means "axe."

- - - - - - - - - - - SNEAKY SABOTAGE - - - - - - - - - - - -

GAS LEAK

N atural gas is an inexpensive, relatively environmentally friendly fuel that has helped millions of people keep warm in the winter—and commit the occasional murder. While the gas is naturally colorless and odorless, providers add sulfur, which smells like rotten eggs, so that people can tell if gas is escaping a contained system. Breathing natural gas in high concentrations starves your brain of oxygen, making you tired and dizzy and giving you a headache. But the real murder comes into play when natural gas, which is amazingly flammable, builds up and ignites. The smallest spark, even from the most innocuous-seeming electronics like a telephone, can blow a gas-filled building sky high.

POP CULTURE Turning an oven on and striking a fire has been a common murderous trope in Hollywood for decades, perhaps most notably in the 1972 film *The Mechanic*, where Charles Bronson plays a hit man who uses this technique to take someone out with a bang.

BOATING ACCIDENT

Boating is dangerous. People legitimately fall overboard, hit their heads, become lost, or get swept out to sea all the time. So it's not exactly unchartered territory to go out for a sail then come back one passenger lighter—accidentally, of course. Drowning, head trauma, and other injuries can all occur from legitimate accidents at sea … but they could also provide cover for a pre-meditated murder. Many murders at sea have been committed both in fiction and in real life. In Patricia Highsmith's dark noir classic *The Talented Mr. Ripley*, Thomas Ripley (played by Matt Damon in the film) murders his man-crush at sea with a boat oar.

KALI LONG KNIVES

The Filipino martial art of Kali (also called Escrima or Arnis) has a deadly weapons curriculum that includes long knives or daggers known as *baraws*. These weapons come in a variety of shapes, sizes, and designs, from the *bolo* (which resembles a machete) to the *kris* (which has a distinctive double-edged wavy "S" blade). Kali practitioners learn to fight with a single long knife or in pairs—slashing, stabbing, and defending with fluidity. There are dozens of deadly long knife techniques in the art; any of which could be used to murder someone by skewering them like human fondue. Yikes!

DEADLY DETAILS **Authentic Kali long knives are intricately made of regional Filipino materials and are widely considered to be beautiful items of Filipino folk art.**

- - - - - - - - - - - - - - - THUG LIFE - - - - - - - - - - - - - - -

COLOMBIAN NECKTIE

This particularly gruesome method of murder involves slitting someone's throat and then, in a most macabre flourish, pulling the victim's tongue through the resulting horizontal wound. I know, right? Yuck. Once a favorite way to dispatch, humiliate, and terrify the enemies of La Cosa Nostra, or the Sicilian mafia, it was later adopted by drug kingpin Pablo Escobar, and gained popularity during the Colombian Civil War between 1978 and 1984. It is commonly associated with organized crime and considered a signature of professional mafia assassins, as well as getting name-checked in the AC/DC song "Dirty Deeds Done Dirt Cheap" (along with "contracts" and "high voltage").

MAC-10

The Military Armament Corporation Model 10, commonly known as the MAC-10, is a compact, American-made machine pistol, designed by Gordon B. Ingram in 1964. The gun is blowback-operated, which means that the force of the cartridge moving backward cycles the weapon. It's built from stamped steel, which keeps the cost down and has contributed to its popularity over the years. Chambered for standard handgun calibers, either .45 ACP or .9mm, the gun quickly grew in popularity when paired with a suppressor. It's a popular gun for urban warfare deployments—and unfortunately, its low cost, high rate of fire and concealableability have also made it popular for urban murder.

POP CULTURE Michael Douglas sports a Mac-10 in his creepy and controversial flip-out film *Falling Down*.

- - - - - - - - - MURDER MOST STRANGE - - - - - - - - -

SEX

Leaving aside STDs, it is possible to actually kill someone simply via sexual intercourse, especially if your partner's heart just isn't up to the task. While uncommon (death during sex is the cause of approximately .06 percent of all sudden deaths), the *Journal of the American Medical Association* says that one hour of sex per week ups the risk of two to three myocardial infarctions and one sudden death by cardiac arrest per 10,000 "person years." And it's not only the act itself that can be fatal. There have been instances around the world where people have been murdered with sex toys, and in 1997, a woman in Los Angeles died after falling from a balcony while having sex with her boss; it was ruled a homicide after it was concluded that he'd pushed her over the railing. Not to mention the elevated cancer risk of the post-coital cigarette!

R*A*PIER

Athin, double-edged sword with origins in 15th-century Spain, the rapier was popular for both civilian and military use. Known to be light and fast, it was used as a fencing weapon perfect for thrusting attacks, peaking in popularity during the 16th and 17th century in Europe. The rapier was also used for self-defense and as a dueling weapon, back when people did such things. In France, the odd duel still occurred with swords like these right up until the 1960s! Today, these swords are popular collectors' items among European Renaissance enthusiasts and hobbyists who enjoy role-playing games.

DEADLY DETAILS **Someone who is especially sharp or observant is known as having a "rapier wit."**

- - - - - - - - - - - - SNEAKY SABOTAGE - - - - - - - - - - - -

GUN CLEANING "ACCIDENTS"

Accidents really do happen when people are maintaining their firearms and fail to do so safely. Between 2005 and 2010, actual gun cleaning accidents killed around 3,800 people. But of course, sometimes these unfortunate events aren't accidents at all. Several murders in the United States were initially reported as gun-cleaning accidents, but later discovered to be something much more sinister. In the cold-blooded murder of one Texas woman in 2002, a man killed his wife and then carefully set up all of the typical trappings of gun cleaning, including newspaper, gun oil and other cleaning supplies. Maybe not a bad idea to have your weapons sent to a professional gunsmith for cleaning!

- - - - - - - - - - - - - - THUG LIFE - - - - - - - - - - - - - -

HANGING

Hanging someone by the neck until dead is a method of murder that's been used since the Middle Ages—oftentimes as state-sponsored execution of a condemned criminal, but also used as a technique of lynch mob violence by vigilantes looking to circumvent reason, legal due process, or just humanity in general. How a hanging is performed will technically affect the victim's manner of death: simply letting a victim hang from a rope will cause death by strangulation, while other variations—such as hanging from a horse then whipping the horse away or letting the body fall several feet until impact—fracture the spinal column instead. Hanging as a means of capital punishment continues to this day. According to Amnesty International, more than fifty countries still hang criminals!

- - - - - - - - - - - - - KILLER MOVES - - - - - - - - - - - - -

KIDNEY PUNCH

Your kidneys are in the middle of your back just below the ribcage. These vital organs serve as a filter for your blood, sifting out toxins. But taking an actual fist to the kidneys can be downright fatal. Punching a kidney can rupture the organ, releasing toxins directly into the bloodstream, or tear it away from the blood vessels it needs to keep going (ew). Numerous deaths have been documented as a result of a hard kidney punch, from the death of a British boxer in the 1900s to the 2007 case of a Russian military policeman who killed a prisoner with a single kidney shot. Kidney punches are illegal in the sport of boxing because of this risk.

- - - - - - - - - - - FATAL FIREARMS - - - - - - - - - - -

HK MP5

The HK MP5 is a high-end, German-made machine pistol (the "HK" in the name stands for Heckler & Koch and the "MP" for *maschinenpistole*) capable of rapid-fire murder all day long. It was designed by a four-man team of engineers and hit the market in 1966, and has since spun off more than 100 variations. The HK MP5 is chambered to fire 9mm ammunition and comes with a 15-round or 30-round magazine capacity. That's a lot of compact firepower! Today, the HK MP5 is one of the most popular submachine guns in the world, seeing service by numerous military and police forces including the United States Navy SEALs, Secret Service, and Federal Bureau of Investigation.

- - - - - - - - - - PERNICIOUS POISONS - - - - - - - - - -

TYLENOL

Throughout history, murderers have used a plethora of exotic and esoteric poisons with which to conduct their shameful trade. But often, some of the most lethal poisons at their disposal are among the most common over-the-counter drugs available. When used as prescribed and instructed by doctors and the manufacturer, Tylenol is a godsend to the general public and medical community. But more than four grams daily of Acetaminophen, the active ingredient in Tylenol, is considered too much. Unfortunately, someone who unknowingly ingests huge quantities of Tylenol is in for big problems—including kidney failure, brain swelling, stroke, heart failure, and death—if treatment isn't sought early on. Tylenol overdose is actually the leading cause of acute liver failure in the United States, leading to hundreds of deaths per year.

- - - - - - - - - MURDER MOST STRANGE - - - - - - - - -

CANNIBALISM

S ince time immemorial, humans have eaten other humans for a variety of reasons, ranging from desperation during times of extreme hunger to celebrating victory over their enemies in combat. But sometimes it's just plain old murder. In modern times, murderers including serial killer Jeffrey Dahmer and abusers of the synthetic drug "bath salts" have stopped for a bite, and in 2012, a Japanese man cut off, cooked, and served his...er...manly bits...to a small group of private diners who paid around $250 for the privilege. How exactly one pairs a wine with that was not reported.

POP CULTURE In 1980, an Italian film depicted cannibals in the Amazon rainforest—instructing cast members who'd supposedly been "eaten" to disappear for a year after the film to appear that they'd died. Cool! Except the Italian courts took it seriously and brought murder charges against the director. The charges were dropped when cast members appeared in court alive and well.

BLUNDERBUSS

The blunderbuss is a wicked little muzzle-loading firearm that dates back to the 17th century. The word "blunderbuss" translates roughly from its original Dutch as "thunder pipe," and the Scandinavian-derived Middle English word meaning "blind." It's a type of early shotgun loaded with smallish lead balls and very effective at short range (as the sheer number of shot pellets meant that one's aim didn't have to be amazing to fire the weapon up close). These guns were typically carried by those on horseback who needed a strong defensive weapon easily manipulated with one hand. In England, carriers of the Royal Mail used blunderbusses to protect their deliveries, and they were also popular with pirates, who knew a thing or two about murder. In addition, famed explorers Lewis and Clark blundered (ahem) their way across the United States armed with several blunderbusses.

KAMA

A *kama* is a traditional Japanese martial arts weapon that resembles a small, single-bladed sickle that can be used with one hand. A common weapon in karate fighting systems, the *kama* was originally a farm implement used to harvest crops by hand. Oftentimes used in pairs, it allows both strong defensive and offensive techniques against other traditional martial arts weapons including swords, staves, and spears. Though most modern martial artists don't farm, they continue to practice with the traditional weapon to honor their arts' cultural roots. In pop culture, the *kama* also commonly appears as a favored weapon of the black-clad ninja warrior—their deadly blades always thirsting for murder.

DEADLY DETAILS **Many martial arts weapons once doubled as farm implements. In feudal Japan, rulers were very stroppy about everyday citizens having weapons—so unless you were a part of the warrior class, you needed an excuse to possess any kind of dangerous tool. (Back then, China, ironically, was much more liberal about weapons ownership.)**

BOWIE KNIFE

The Bowie Knife is a large, fixed-blade personal fighting knife with a single straight edge, a small hilt, and a wooden handle. The weapon's namesake was Jim Bowie—a rough-and-tumble 19th century American pioneer and hero at the Battle of the Alamo during the Texas Revolution. The original design for the knife is actually credited to Jim Bowie's brother, Rezin, but Jim first made the knife famous during a Louisiana duel, and later went on to refine the design. Today the Bowie Knife is popular across the American South, or any state with tractor pulls and a taste for chicken fried steak.

INDUSTRIAL ACCIDENT

The office can be a dangerous place, especially when not everyone is looking out for your wellbeing. The intentional murder of somebody in the workplace, disguised as just another day at the office, is older than the Industrial Revolution itself. Over the years, coworkers have killed each other on the job for a variety of reasons from professional jealousy to love triangles—using forklifts, arson, heavy machinery, trucks, and accidental "falls." These days, most people's daily work is less physically dangerous on the whole, therefore, dying on the job for any reason is considerably less common—though the phenomenon of crazed coworkers snapping could happen in any cubicle. So it can't hurt to bring donuts once in a while or take the time to at least act interested in those vacation photos.

ANTIFREEZE

Talk about cold blooded. Antifreeze is that greenish-yellow stuff your car uses to keep the engine cool; its chemical properties both lower water's freezing point and raise its boiling point so drivers in different climates can conveniently maintain their engines. Unfortunately, some of those people are also driven to murder. Antifreeze is extremely poisonous to both people and animals, and its victims do not go gently into that good night. Basically a mixture of water and alcohol, its main ingredient is often ethylene glycol, which has a sweet taste when ingested but causes acute kidney failure. It's been used by so many (now convicted) poisoners in recent decades that investigators now always test for ethylene glycol in suspected poisoning cases when something doesn't seem right.

DEADLY DETAILS Because of its danger to people and animals, **alternative antifreeze formulas are now being manufactured that deliver the same chemical properties in a safer way. It's about time!**

- - - - - - - - - MURDER MOST STRANGE - - - - - - - - -
ZOMBIFICATION

In popular science fiction, zombies have served as metaphors for everything from communism or socialism to mindless consumerism. But they have an actual basis in real life—and real murder! With origins in the Vodun (voodoo) religion, zombification was well-known in Haiti as a situation where a person's "soul" was separated from the physical body. The process remains scientifically fuzzy and widely debated, but is said to have involved giving victims a non-fatal dose of natural toxins and hallucinogens, leaving them in a perpetual state of confusion. However performed, zombification is still considered a form of murder in Haiti, even if the victim continues—technically—to live.

DEADLY DETAILS There is a suggestive element as well, and **alternative theories used to explain modern "zombies" range from brain damage to mental illness.**

TOMMY GUN

The Thompson submachine gun, popularly known as the Tommy Gun, was one of the first automatic weapons to see widespread military and civilian service in the United States. Not to mention, widespread murder. Shooting a .45 ACP round, the Tommy Gun saw service in World War I trench warfare and helped keep pace with German advancements in automatic weaponry. But it soon became infamous for its widespread use by Prohibition Era gangsters in the 1920s; the matching fedora, cigar and violin case becoming *de rigueur.* It continued to see military service in World War II and beyond, and today is a popular item among firearm collectors.

BROADSWORD

A broadsword is a generalized term for any heavy, double-edged early military sword used in field combat. Typically basket-hilted (with a rounded cage covering the handle and protecting the hand) and sporting a straight blade, it's sharpened on the end and two sides, designed to cut and thrust. Its broad, flat blade is what gives it both its name and its long legacy of murder. What most people think of as a broadsword is the kind of sword one sees carried by knights in movies set during Medieval times—though numerous cultures around the world have produced their own versions of the broadsword. The *Highlander* movie franchise, Renaissance Faires, and role-playing gamers keep up interest in the broadsword; some people actually still learn to fight with these primitive weapons from back in the day.

TOILET

While not exactly a murder method found in the classic detective game *Clue*, people *have* been murdered via toilet. It's an especially common method in prisons, when dangerous people may be locked up together in a small space with nothing but … well … a toilet. But it happens outside of prisons too: in 2014, a Brazilian man was killed by a falling toilet during the

World Cup, when soccer fans ripped toilets out of the stadium and hurled them over the side onto the street (and one unfortunate victim). The number one way to be killed with a toilet is from forcible drowning. Which is not only pretty crappy behavior, but also most assuredly flushes your future down the drain.

TRUE CRIME In addition, murders have been *sparked* by the toilet—such as the Florida man who killed his roommate in 2006 because they were out of toilet paper.

STAIR "FALL"

Arranging for someone to "accidentally" fall down the stairs has been the method of many a murder, though it's amazing how many pushy little killers think themselves too clever to be caught. It's tricky, though, because so many people do actually fall down the stairs without help—a million people a year are injured and more than 10,000 people per year die from it. The most common fatal injuries involve hitting one's head, breaking important bones, or, for the elderly or infirm, causing minor injuries that lead to bigger complications. How do you avoid being the victim of such an attack? One step at a time.

POP CULTURE The movies *Vertigo, Casino Royale, Die Hard, The Shining* and *The Bourne Identity* all had deadly down-the-stairs scenes.

- - - - - - - - - - PERNICIOUS POISONS - - - - - - - - - -

CYANOGEN CHLORIDE

This chemical concoction, commonly known as CK, is a terrifying gas once developed for use in chemical warfare, though it also has a number of non-murderous industrial applications (such as in laboratories, for various scientific processes). Just one of many dreadful chemical weapons covered by the Chemical Weapons Convention, CK is produced through the oxidation of sodium cyanide with chlorine, and when released as a chemical weapon, acts as a deadly blood agent that can pass through the various common filters on military and civilian gas masks. The victims on the receiving end of a CK gas attack experience all manner of horrific symptoms, ranging from coughing to paralysis and death. Interestingly (and disgustingly), low levels of cyanogen chloride can be created by peeing in a chlorinated swimming pool. Enjoy your Marco Polo.

- - - - - - - - - - - **FATAL FIREARMS** - - - - - - - - - - -

FN FAL

Manufactured by the Belgian arms maker Fabrique Nationale de Herstal (FN), the Fusil Automatique Léger, or FAL, translates to "Light Automatic Rifle." This military rifle is one of the world's deadliest. Originally chambered for 7.62x51, this durable gas-operated weapon came with a 20-to-30-round magazine capacity and the ability to fire selectively or on full auto. The standard FN FAL can fire a blistering 650 to 700 rounds of murderous hot lead per minute. First used by the Nazis during WWII, it also saw service in the UK, and later around the world from Venezuela to Vietnam.

DEADLY DETAILS **Throughout the 20th century, dozens of variants on this successful rifle were developed around the world such as the Olin/Winchester FAL and the Sturmgewehr 58.**

- - - - - - - - - - - - - **THUG LIFE** - - - - - - - - - - - - -

DRAWING AND QUARTERING

To be drawn and quartered was a brutal form of capital punishment whereby the condemned was dragged by horse to the gallows, hanged until not-quite-dead, then taken down, emasculated, disemboweled, beheaded, and chopped into four separate parts. Talk about freakin' overkill! This was the punishment for treason in "jolly old" England from the 1200s to the 1800s. Oftentimes, the victim's remains would be put on public display across the kingdom in iconic locations such as London Bridge; this was done to discourage others from committing similar acts. Sounds pretty discouraging.

DEADLY DETAILS **Probably the most famous committer of treason to suffer this fate was Guy Fawkes, who attempted to assassinate King James on November 5, 1604 with a plot to blow up Parliament. Today, Britons worldwide celebrate Guy Fawkes Day every November 5th with bonfires, parties, and fireworks.**

- - - - - - - - - - - - - KILLER MOVES - - - - - - - - - - - - - -

THREE-SECTIONED STAFF

The three-sectioned staff is a traditional Chinese martial arts weapon composed of three lengths of pole connected by chain or rope. This weapon, which was historically made of wax wood (from the Chinese privet tree), may be employed by a martial artist to defend against a variety of weapons—and attack at a variety of ranges in a number of different ways. It can even be used to disarm an opponent using its chains or being clever with how you manipulate the sections. A complex weapon to master, it was first studied widely by disciples of the Shaolin temple thousands of years ago. The three-sectioned staff is much more concealable than comparable weapons, making it perfect for self-protection back in the day. Or murder.

BOOT KNIFE

As advertised, a boot knife is a small straight knife worn hidden in a boot or attached to one's ankle. Just the ticket for personal defense—or murder! These knives have a fixed blade and are typically double-edged. During the 20th century, they were common among soldiers in the field; probably the most iconic version for military fieldwork was the British-designed Fairbairn-Sykes commando knife, which was a long boot knife that saw action with Allied forces during WWII and beyond.

DEADLY DETAILS During America's pioneer times, boot knives were so popular with gamblers (used as an ace-in-the-hole if things really went downhill during a game) that they were also known as "gambler's daggers."

SLIPPERY SURFACE

It's totally possible to murder somebody by making a floor, staircase, or other surface so slippery as to be unsafe. Greasing up a window cleaner's scaffolding, purposely icing the deck of an arctic fishing vessel, or just plain wetting down the floor unexpectedly can absolutely get someone killed. While death isn't a foregone conclusion after a slip and fall, a killer's evil intention could easily lead to a poor, unsuspecting victim's death. Hundreds of people slip and kill themselves in the bathtub alone every year—and that's without any help from the unscrupulous.

ANTHRAX

nthrax is a fiendishly deadly disease caused by a bacteria known as *Bacillus anthracis*, which conventionally infects plant-eating animals. Cows, sheep, or vegetarians who graze on plants tainted with the bacteria begin to get cold or flu symptoms, then pneumonia—and then, if left untreated, keel over dead. Sometimes just breathing in the spores is enough; even eating an animal that itself consumed a high number of spores could be trouble. That's why certain strains of anthrax are employed as a biological weapon by those hell-bent on murder.

DEADLY DETAILS The disease is spread by endospores which can stay active and dangerous for centuries!

BOOMERANG

urder by boomerang is a terrible idea, because what goes around, comes around! (Rimshot.) Originally a hunting implement of Australia's aboriginal people, these flat and angular wooden weapons have been said to have seen use for the last 10,000 years! Its shape is such that it flies in an arc—returning to the user after a brief flight. Actual death from a boomerang shot would be caused by trauma (not as a result of a cut, as in the famous *Mad Max: Road Warrior* boomerang scenes), most likely to the head. Still, the phenomenon of boomerang murder is a lot more common in Sherlock Holmes stories and on television than in real life, where boomerangs are mostly used to murder one's free time.

REMINGTON MODEL 870

The Remington Model 870 is an American-made pump action shotgun. Designed in 1949, the Remington 870 comes in a variety of gauges, and some of the high-end tactical varieties carry up to eight shots at once. Most police forces in the developed world employ Remington shotguns as part of their service arsenal. One of the most popular shotguns in the world with more than 10 million made, and used by everyone from duck hunters to SWAT teams, odds are high that at least one's been employed for murder.

DEADLY DETAILS Chinese gun maker Norinco makes knock-off versions of these weapons that are scary cheap.

- - - - - - - - - - - SLASHER MADNESS - - - - - - - - - - -

GHURKA

A "ghurka" (or "kukri") is a long, angled knife resembling a machete with a blade that juts off at in inward angle in the middle and a handle conventionally made of buffalo horn or some kind of hard wood. A traditional weapon in the country of Nepal, some of the oldest surviving relics date back to the 1500s. The Nepalese people used these tools in everyday life, primarily for chopping—but they're also well suited for fighting (and killing). It's popularly known as a "ghurka" in the west because of its adoption by Britain's Royal Gurkha Rifles, an elite fighting force that recruited from a town in Nepal called "Gorkha." The Gurkhas have gained a reputation as some of the world's toughest infantrymen, making this design of knife popular worldwide.

51

VENOMOUS SPIDERS

I t's possible to kill somebody by placing highly venomous spiders someplace where the arachnids are likely to bite the victim. Psychopathic dictator Pol Pot was said to put venomous spiders in the wounds of his prisoners—what a swell fellow. If someone were set on murder-via-spider, their best bets, based on the potency of the spiders' venom, would probably be either Brazilian Wander Spiders, Black or Brown Widows, Brown Recluses, or Chinese Bird Spiders. The world's most painful spider? By far *The Amazing Spider-Man 2* film starring Andrew Garfield, which most critics say causes two hours and 22 minutes' worth of undeniable agony.

POP CULTURE In the James Bond film *Dr. No*, the beautiful Honey Ryder, played by Ursula Andress, was said to have killed a man by placing a deadly spider in his bed.

- -

DIM MAK

The phrase "dim mak" translates from Chinese to mean "death touch," and refers to any martial art strike that is said to kill an opponent by hitting a specific and sensitive target. If that's not murder, what is?! While modern evidence of the veracity of dim mak claims is shaky, the idea is widely used in Chinese Wuxia films and novels—fantastical tales of love, magic, kung fu, morality, and adventure set in olden day China. There are also some modern day martial arts instructors who claim to teach dim mak techniques, but they are widely regarded as hucksters.

DEADLY DETAILS **Dim mak is not to be confused with dim sum, which is not murderous, but delicious.**

FALLING OBJECT

Though it seems like something from a Bugs Bunny cartoon, people are killed by falling objects all the time: construction workers killed by falling tools, materials, and equipment; city folk killed by falling televisions; country people by falling trees; mountaineers by falling boulders; and islanders by falling coconuts. In 1988, a New York man was killed by an air conditioner that fell from the seventh floor of a building. In 2014, a Chicago woman was killed by a decorative metal gargoyle that fell from a church. And in Turkey, a goat jumped from the roof of a building and killed a person on the street. So do yourself a favor and look up from that cell phone once in a while.

THUG LIFE
BEHEADING

"**O**ff with his head!" A method of murder from the days of yore, beheading (decapitation) involves simply cutting off some poor soul's head, resulting in almost instantaneous death, since the brain dies almost immediately without the circulation of oxygenated blood. Throughout much of history, beheading has been used as a form of government-sanctioned capital punishment, popular because of its highly public and intimidating nature. Many a royal or head of state went to their death in this fashion; more than one of King Henry VIII's wives lost their lives this way, and Queen Elizabeth I had her cousin, Mary Queen of Scots, beheaded because Mary served as a threat to Elizabeth's crown.

DEADLY DETAILS Interestingly, some creatures can live quite some time headless. A cockroach, for example, will die if its head is removed—but only from starvation. Which makes them somehow even creepier than they already are.

MURDER MOST STRANGE
DEATH BY VOLCANO

If you've got one handy, a volcano can be a great murder weapon. Hard to conceal, sure, but on the other hand? Zero evidence in terms of a corpse, since a human body will instantly vaporize upon contact with the extreme temperatures present in an active volcano. (The hottest types of lava, molten andesite and basalt, top out at around 2,190 degrees Fahrenheit! That's pretty darn deadly.) In times past, some cultures have sacrificed virgins for religious purposes; the remains of Incan children have been found on the upper slopes of the Andes in South America. But this practice wasn't as widespread as Hollywood would have you believe, if for no other reason than that the shape and phase of most volcanoes doesn't actually resemble a boiling pot of lava.

- - - - - - - - - - - **PERNICIOUS POISONS** - - - - - - - - - - -

RICIN

R icin is a super-deadly protein found in the seeds of castor oil plants. It's so toxic, that just a few grains of the stuff can be fatal, and it's most fatal when inhaled. Once inside the body, ricin prevents cells from metabolizing. It's possible to survive a ricin attack, but those who do will likely have long-term organ damage. Because of its ease of manufacture, ricin has been employed by a number of nefarious groups. Talk about scary stuff!

DEADLY DETAILS **The U.S. government once researched using ricin as a deadly applicant to bullets and shrapnel, but it never saw widespread practice, although weaponized ricin was used in cluster bombs during WWII.**

- - - - - - - - - - - - - - **THUG LIFE** - - - - - - - - - - - - - - -

BASEBALL BAT

B aseball may be America's official pastime, but over the years the baseball bat has gained a reputation on the street for ad hoc violence and, of course, murder. Baseball bats are traditionally popular weapons because they're pretty cheap, pretty easy to get, and pretty innocuous. Their rep for makeshift murder dates to Prohibition-

Era gangster Al Capone, who was famous for using a baseball bat to crack heads on the job. Both the baseball bat and the legal term describing the crime of battery are derived from the French *batter*, meaning "to strike."

POP CULTURE The sport of baseball dates back to before the Civil War, but it wasn't as omnipresent as it is today. Cricket was once very popular in the United States, and a number of regional baseball variations existed over the years as the sport developed.

- - - - - - - - - - - FATAL FIREARMS - - - - - - - - - - -

GLOCK 22

One of the most popular weapons among American law enforcement today is the Glock 22, a .40 caliber semi-automatic handgun first introduced in 1990. With a 15-round standard magazine capacity (and an optional aftermarket 22-round magazine), the Glock 22 is amazingly durable and reliable. It is the standard issue sidearm for the U.S. Drug Enforcement Agency, Delta Force, the FBI, the U.S. Marshals and the Bureau of Alcohol, Tobacco, Firearms and Explosives. (Tommy Lee Jones sported a Glock 22 in the 1998 action movie *U.S. Marshals*.) With such a lethal reputation, it was bound to be noticed by those with less-than-honorable intentions. Such as, you know, murder.

- - - - - - - - - - - SLASHER MADNESS - - - - - - - - - - -

BUCK KNIFE

Company founder and blade-smith Hoyt Buck was a blacksmith's apprentice in Kansas before settling into a career making handmade hunting knives from his home in Idaho. He made a number of different knife designs, including fixed-blade knives for use by soldiers during WWII (which he donated to them for free). But it was owning one of his 1964 Buck Folding Hunter knives that became a rite of passage for sportsmen. Unsurprisingly, with all of those boys and all of those blades, somebody was bound to lose his temper. Sadly, Buck knives have been used in multiple murders including the grizzly killing of Sharon Tate by the Manson family. Mr. Buck would have gravely disapproved.

POP CULTURE In the cheesy 1970s TV show *The Dukes of Hazzard*, Bo and Luke Duke each carried a Buck model 110— but all they killed were 1969 model Dodge Chargers.

- - - - - - - - - - - SNEAKY SABOTAGE - - - - - - - - - - -

HIT-AND-RUN

Motorcars first hit the streets in the early twentieth century, and it wasn't long before they also hit some unfortunate bystanders who happened to be in the wrong place at the wrong time. In most cases, this was entirely accidental. But sometimes, of course, it was entirely murder. Back in the day, there were far fewer cars, yet if a pedestrian was struck by a vehicle, it was often quite tricky to discover the culprit should the guilty party not want to be found. Drivers of old wore goggles and didn't have license plates. So unless witnesses happened to know the driver by sight, there wasn't much for investigators to work with. Today there are more than a billion cars on the road, but advances in governance and technology mean that the perpetrator of a hit-and-run is much more likely to be caught, or at least identified. About one in five pedestrians killed on the streets are victims of hit-and-run motor vehicle crashes.

CHUCK NORRIS

Nuclear weapons. Elite special forces. Aircraft carriers. America has at its disposal many deadly weapons, but so few widely feared and respected as Chuck Norris. Known for his martial arts action roles in dozens of movies and television shows from *Return of the Dragon* to *Walker, Texas Ranger*, just pointing Chuck Norris in someone's general direction may be enough to stop their heart from sheer fright. Norris began his career as a successful martial artist first (practicing the Korean art of Tang Soo Do), and was encouraged to start acting by Steve McQueen in the late '60s. In 2010, Norris was made an honorary Texas Ranger.

FLAMETHROWER

While not exactly stealthy, flamethrowers were literally made for murder. Whether worn as a pack, mounted on a truck, or shot from a tank, flamethrowers are weapons created as a means of overcoming enemy entrenchments. The German military developed the modern flamethrower during WWI to terrorize and neutralize enemy combatants hiding in defensive trench positions. A surprising number of modern killers have adopted this gruesome and complex weapon, including a 2008 case where a California man dressed as Santa Claus killed nine people at a family Christmas party by wielding a homemade flame thrower wrapped as a Christmas present. Ho, ho, ho!

DEADLY DETAILS **Oddly, flamethrowers are legal for citizens to own in the United States.**

MACHETE

The machete is a large, long knife native to tropical countries and used in farming, to clear away brush. Most machetes have a sharp edge and a flat edge, and are composed of a single piece of steel for a blade, a long tang (part of the blade that's embedded in the handle), and a simple handle of wood or composite. From hacking away rainforests to cutting open coconuts, you'll find machetes around the globe from Africa to South America—which is why they're also so terribly convenient for murder, revolution, jungle warfare, and other messy endeavors.

POP CULTURE As a murder weapon, the machete rose to fame as the implement of choice for the fictional killer of confused lakeside teenagers in the campy *Friday the 13th* movie series, which debuted in 1980s yet keeps trying to kill our evenings with sequels.

HYDROGEN SULFIDE

T he chemical compound H$_2$S is an extremely hazardous gas that is absolutely capable of killing. Hydrogen sulfide smells like rotten eggs, and is found in natural gas, crude oil, hot water springs, and in places like swamps where organic matter or sewage decompose. It can also be an industrial byproduct of oil and gas drilling and refining, paper mills, and other manufacturing activities. In very low concentrations, someone exposed to H$_2$S may merely cough or get itchy eyes. But in higher concentrations? We're talking about death from just a single breath! And if that weren't murderous enough, H$_2$S is also highly flammable and can explode.

TRUE CRIME **H$_2$S has been used to solve crimes as well. In 1829, when forensic technology was still nascent, investigators used H$_2$S as a tool to detect arsenic in a real-life cup of poisoned coffee used by a grandson to kill his grandfather over the inheritance of a country farm in England.**

SAUNA/STEAM BATH

A nice stop by the sauna can melt away the stress of the day. But too much of a good thing means your days could be numbered! Saunas come in many designs around the world, but basically all do the same thing: provide an enclosed space that heats up and makes you pleasantly sweaty. Stay in a sauna too long, however, whether by your own free will or by being locked in with murderous intent, and your body soon becomes unable to manage sauna-levels of heat. Dehydration, low blood pressure, organ failure, and—eventually—death by heart attack can follow.

POP CULTURE In the 2011 horror movie *247°F*, weekenders are locked in a hot sauna fighting to survive—without any bottled water or even *The New York Times* crossword!

- - - - - - - - - - - SNEAKY SABOTAGE - - - - - - - - - - - -

"FAULTY" HOUSE WIRING

Murder by arson, specifically by deliberately causing a household electrical problem, is both reprehensible and tricky to troubleshoot forensically. Modern homes are crammed with live electrical currents, which is great when everything is working the right way. But in the hands of the wrong person, all of this convenience can be downright deadly. The average home in the United States is wired with 120V wiring which can, if wired incorrectly or using dysfunctional components, spark an instant fire that puts lives and property at risk. Arson investigators are trained to forensically uncover the root of a blaze, but since legitimate faulty wiring is so common it could be difficult to identify when the "mistake" was intentionally created by a murderous third party. Either way it still means lights-out for the poor victims.

- - - - - - - - - - - FATAL FIREARMS - - - - - - - - - - - -

TAURUS JUDGE

Forjas Taurus, a Brazilian gun manufacturer, makes this five-shot revolver, which can shoot both .45-caliber bullets *and* .410 shotgun shells (most firearms can only fire one caliber of ammunition).

Legally considered a short-barreled shotgun in California (and banned in that state), this murderous little pistol earned its name when the judges in high-crime areas of Miami, Florida began packing them for personal protection in the courtroom. Judges are also popular vehicle weapons in urban areas where people are concerned about carjacking, and in rural areas where folks are concerned about wild snakes. Of course, while made with the best of intentions, it's also capable of plain old-fashioned, up-close murder. In 2011, members of a nut ball anti-government militia in Georgia used a Taurus Judge to shoot and kill two teenagers who'd discovered the group's ridiculous plan to assassinate the President and overthrow the U.S. government.

- - - - - - - - - - - SLASHER MADNESS - - - - - - - - - -

MEAT CLEAVER

A meat cleaver resembles a small, square hatchet and is used to do heavy lifting in the kitchen and at the butcher's, since it will cut not only through meat but also bone. Relying on brute mechanical force, they aren't super-sharp—their typical grind is only about 25 degrees. In fact, if they're too sharp, they'll chip—or you'll spend all day trying to pry it out of your cutting board. The cleaver doesn't care whether it's cutting through a New York strip steak or … something else. Which is what makes it so gruesomely perfect for murder.

TRUE CRIME **The meat cleaver is reputedly the preferred weapon of the notorious Chinese "Triad" gang, which runs organized crime operations around the world. In 2013, an alleged Triad crime boss got a taste of his own medicine (or just the wrath of an angry coworker) when he was disemboweled with a meat cleaver.**

SHAOLIN MONK'S SPADE

A monk's spade is a long metal pole with a large crescent moon-shaped blade on one end and a smaller, similar blade on the other. Large and intimidating, these flashy weapons have murder written all over them, and are hugely popular in both contemporary and classic kung fu movies. But with such a heavy and hard-to-use weapon, the user almost certainly needs a year or two of formal training lest they murder themselves by accident.

DEADLY DETAILS A traditional Chinese martial arts weapon originating from the Shaolin temple, these weapons served as both functional shovels (to bury unfortunate souls according to Buddhist tradition) and as a means of self-defense.

SHOES

W hen a murderer snaps, they tend to use whatever weapon is handy. And no matter where you are, most people tend to have a pair of shoes around. In 2014, a woman in Houston, Texas was convicted of fatally stabbing her boyfriend in the face twenty-five times with a size 9 five-and-a-half-inch stiletto heel. It's also possible to murder someone by strangling them with a shoestring (which is why you have to remove them in jail, and why criminal wannabes don't wear them in their sneakers—emulating jailhouse culture). May God have mercy on your sole.

GLOCK 17

Glock is an Austrian maker of precision firearms, specializing in polymer semi-automatic pistols. The Glock 17 is the full-size 9mm model which holds seventeen shots; more than five million of these reliable and versatile handguns have been made. Because of their ease-of-use, many firearms schools and gun ranges use Glock 17 handguns when instructing men and women new to shooting. Lightweight, easy to clean, and super-reliable, these guns are so well-made and affordable that over half of the police officers in the United States carry Glock pistols—although among gun enthusiasts, some detractors uncomfortable with the Glock's polymer construction refer to the guns as: "Tactical Tupperware."

SAWED-OFF SHOTGUN

This modified shotgun is one where the owner hacks off the barrel to make it shorter, thereby making it both a more dangerous short-range weapon and more easily concealed. You have to cut a shotgun down pretty short—at least halving the barrel length—before it begins to affect how big a pattern your shot makes (that is, before the shorter barrel gives you a wider spread). Most people associate short-barreled shotguns with criminals and criminal activities, since many nations and states have outlawed these modified shotguns. However, some military and law enforcement groups also employ these weapons in tactical situations where space is limited and carrying a long-barreled tactical shotgun is impractical. But no matter who's wielding one, you don't want to be on the business end.

DRIVE-BY SHOOTING

This tragic form of murder happens all too often in many of the world's biggest cities—especially in the United States. Often gang-related, these murderous acts involve shooting a gun from a moving vehicle into someone's home, business, car, or person. Oftentimes, these events occur in a murderous cycle—with one gang committing a drive-by shooting against another party and then the victim's gang affiliates committing a similar crime to settle the score.

DEADLY DETAILS **As if the drive-by shooter's murderous intent wasn't bad enough, often innocent bystanders are the ones killed instead of the intended victims. One study during the 1990s in Los Angeles revealed that between 38 and 59 percent of drive-by shooting victims were innocent bystanders.**

BAD PRESCRIPTION

Giving the wrong medication, denying someone necessary medicine, or prescribing the wrong dosage can all add up to murder. That's why a doctor's ability to prescribe medication is so regulated, and why pharmacists undergo rigorous training and licensing. The death of pop icon Michael Jackson was attributed to an inappropriate prescription of anesthetic by Houston doctor Conrad Murray, who was eventually convicted of involuntary manslaughter. In the Christmas classic *It's a Wonderful Life*, a young George Bailey prevents his boss, Old Man Gower, from accidentally delivering the wrong medication to a patient. The legal term for such a foul-up is pharmaceutical malpractice or pharmaceutical negligence. More than 100,000 people die each year from adverse reactions to getting the wrong drug or dose.

HAYMAKER

A "haymaker" is slang for a wild, technically inefficient, roundhouse punch that's meant to knock out your opponent. It's called a haymaker because the wide, swinging motion resembles somebody using a scythe—a traditional farming tool used to harvest hay. Hitting someone with a haymaker is considered a desperate act, sort of like a Hail Mary pass in football. In the movies, people get punched in the head all the time and keep going as if nothing ever happened. In real life, however, punching someone in the head with a full-on haymaker can kill them.

NUCLEAR BOMB

As the most fearsome weapon of mass destruction in the world, there is no more infamous a murder weapon as the use of nuclear fission to create super-deadly military ordnance. The earliest nuclear bombs were developed as a result of the Manhattan Project during WWII—leading to the horrific atomic bombs dropped by the Americans on Hiroshima and Nagasaki in Japan. Proliferation of nuclear weapons ramped up during the Cold War, but receded in the face of widespread anti-nuclear sentiment.

THUG LIFE - - - - - - - - - - -

BARE-HANDED STRANGLING

Technically, strangling can occur using a noose, garrote, or other implement—but when most people say "strangling," they mean choking someone with their bare hands. Choking a victim cuts off the supplies of oxygen and blood to the victim's brain, causing first unconsciousness and then death. Ten percent of violent deaths in the United States every year are due to strangulation. Since *Homo sapiens* have always had hands, we've always been capable of this brutal method of murder. Still, while many people may claim at one time or another that they could murder someone with their bare hands, very few people actually mean it. Yikes!

TRUE CRIME Jack the Ripper would often strangle his victims to death before performing his other unspeakable trademark defilements. The serial killer (or killers) known as the Boston Strangler often straggled victims with panty hose.

- - - - - - - - - - **PERNICIOUS POISONS** - - - - - - - - -

CURARE

Talk about murderous! Curare is a super-deadly alkaloid plant toxin that grows as a large vine found in the Central and South American rainforest, harvested by using the leaves and roots of the plant. The natives of South America once used it to coat their poisoned arrows or blowgun darts; since the poison only works when introduced into the victim's bloodstream, they could use curare-tipped arrows to hunt large mammals yet still eat the meat without getting sick themselves. Exposure to the toxin means failure of the large muscles and eventually death by asphyxiation, when the muscles in the diaphragm fail. However, curare was once administered in small doses as a muscle relaxant during abdominal surgeries.

- - - - - - - - - - - - FATAL FIREARMS - - - - - - - - - - - -
DERRINGER

A derringer is a general term for a pocket-sized handgun. The phrase came about as a result of the popular micro-pistols Henry Deringer manufactured in Philadelphia during the 1800s. (For some reason, when the phrase came to reference small guns in general, people began misspelling Deringer with two "R's.") Deringer's original guns were muzzle-loading and held just one shot. These tiny guns were popular with ladies, because they could be hidden in a handbag—and, of course, also easily concealed for murderers. Deringer's guns became so popular that numerous people copied his designs illegally, and he spent his whole life fighting legal battles to protect his intellectual property.

TRUE CRIME **John Wilkes Booth used a derringer handgun to assassinate President Abraham Lincoln.**

- - - - - - - - - - - - - KILLER MOVES - - - - - - - - - - - - -
MANTIS FIST

T his deadly kung fu style is known as the Tang Lang, or Praying Mantis Kung Fu Style. With its origins in the Shaolin temple of ancient China, Praying Mantis uses whip-like aggressive techniques to rain down blow after blow on an opponent. And the result can be killer! In the old days, kung fu masters used to challenge each other; the winner would gain the public's respect and more students would flock to him. The loser…well…didn't always make it. The 1978 movie *Death Duel of the Mantis* shows the mantis fist in deadly action.

DEADLY DETAILS There are actually two distinct families of Praying Mantis Kung Fu—one originating from Northern China and another created by the Hakka people of the south.

- - - - - - - - - - **PERNICIOUS POISONS** - - - - - - - - - -
RHODODENDRONS

These beautiful flowers bloom in late spring, producing awesome colorful explosions of pink, white, red, purple, and yellow flowers and attracting hummingbirds. Oh, but pretty as they are, every part of this plant is toxic. The leaves are the worst, containing high levels of a potentially fatal poison called grayanotoxin—which at significant doses can cause sweating, vomiting, low blood pressure, heart problems, and occasionally death. Grayanotoxin can also be found in tainted honey, so called "mad honey." Keep rhododendrons away from cats and dogs, too, as they're even more likely to die from its toxins than humans. The good news is, with 700 species of rhododendrons in the world, not all contain grayanotoxin. Not that you'll want to take the chance.

POP CULTURE In the 2009 *Sherlock Holmes* remake with Robert Downey, Jr., a "hydrated rhododendron" is used to paralyze one of the characters.

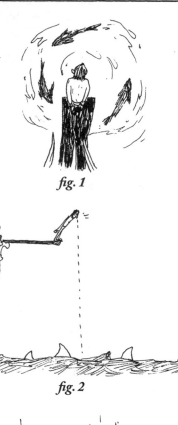

fig. 1

fig. 2

fig. 3

WALKING the PLANK

A terrifying form of murder at sea, "walking the plank" was used to both kill and torture. The practice dates back to the 1700s, and was most often used by mutineers, pirates, or other maritime criminals. The victim would be bound, and perhaps weighted, then made to walk a board extended over the side of a ship. If you've ever sailed in open waters and stared into the vast nothingness of a cold ocean, you can imagine the terror. Tales of walking the plank abounded in 1700s English literature and continue to fuel swashbuckling pirate tales to this day. Walking the plank was part punishment, but also part sadistic entertainment by criminals on the water. Talk about being sick at sea.

FOXGLOVE

Digitalis purpurea, known as "foxglove," is a beautiful, flowering ornamental shrub. Its tall spikes of trumpet-shaped flowers bloom in long rows and in a variety of colors. It's a striking plant when it's in bloom. The only downside? These beauties are totally toxic. Eating any part of this flower can kill you—even in small amounts. The plant contains cardiac glycosides, which damage the heart, as well as other toxins that lead to a stomach ache, irregular pulse, convulsions, and, eventually, death.

TRUE CRIME Serial killer Charles Cullen used a substance derived from foxglove to kill around 40 people during his stint as a nurse in Pennsylvania and New Jersey.

- - - - - - - - - - - SNEAKY SABOTAGE - - - - - - - - - - -

AUTO "ACCIDENT"

According to the World Health Organization, about 1.24 million people per year die in auto accidents. So it can be hard to tell when one of them, well, isn't an accident at all. In one Australian case, a young man murdered his parents by smothering them, then rolling their car off an embankment to collect inheritance. Many British conspiracy theorists think that Princess Diana's fatal car accident was in reality an assassination. While the specific number of real-life cases like this is unknown, the number of novels and movies that use this murder method in the plot are numerous—including *The Postman Always Rings Twice*, *Patriot Games*, *Blow Out*, and *Dolores Claiborne*.

LASERS

Y ou could totally murder somebody with a laser (and not just by using the laser sight of a handgun). Even low-powered lasers can blind someone for life, and high-powered lasers can be used to shoot down rockets. But most people don't have the kind of super-powered laser handy to do such a thing. Deadly lasers would be so huge as to be impractical; but while instances of murder-by-laser are scarce, there was a big rumor going around that former Prime Minister of Pakistan Benazir Bhutto was assassinated by a laser.

DEADLY DETAILS **A laser is a device that amplifies and emits light; in fact, its name is an acronym for Light Amplification Stimulated Emission of Radiation.**

URBAN RIOT

A s cultural and economic centers, living in a big city can be awesome. Of course, they can also be dangerous! With all of those people living on top of one another, tempers are bound to flare every once in a while. And when violence spreads like a wildfire, it's a perfect backdrop for murder. Events like the 2011 "BlackBerry riots," in England (so named because they were organized via social media) or the 1992 riots in Los Angeles are examples of deadly urban violence. Sixty people were killed over a five-day period during those LA riots; many of the murders remain unsolved. In the epic 1983 gangster classic *Scarface*, the movie opens up with the staged killing of a Cuban politician by first inciting a riot as a distraction.

BROWNING HI-POWER

The Browning Hi-Power is a semi-automatic handgun first designed by renowned American gunsmith John Browning, and put into service in the French military during the 1930s. Its capacity to kill was well proven during WWII, when it was used as a sidearm by both the Axis and Allied forces. Though considered an old-fashioned design today, the Browning Hi-Power handgun remains capable of murder, and is actually still used as a military service pistol in India, Indonesia, Venezuela, and other countries.

DEADLY DETAILS **The Browning Hi-Power's design shares some similarities to the 1911 pistol, which Browning also created.**

- - - - - - - - - - SLASHER MADNESS - - - - - - - - - - -

LIPSTICK KNIFE

This killer cosmetic looks like an ordinary tube of lipstick on the outside, but take the cap off and you'll reveal a small (one- or two-inch) sharp blade that can be the kiss of death. These deadly beauties have been in existence since at least the Cold War, and possibly much earlier. These weapons aren't legal in many places, and bringing one on an airplane will certainly kill your chances of boarding the flight. These days, a not-so-innocent tube of lipstick can also hide stun guns, mace, and actual firearms.

DEADLY DETAILS **The practice of applying lipstick dates back to ancient Egypt, so it's likely that clever blade-smiths throughout the ages have given ladies an extra edge.**

MOTORCYCLE ACCIDENT

I f you ride a motorcycle, your odds of dying on it without help from anyone else are already thirty-four times greater than riding in any other type of vehicle. It's easy to get into a tough spot quickly when you're out on the open road—cars and trucks might not see you and could pull right out in front of you, and there's not much between the person and the pavement. So while murder via motorcycle accident would be an awful thing to happen to any poor soul, it wouldn't be terribly tough to pull off from a technical standpoint—though premeditated murder is much less common than those stemming from road rage or reckless driving under the influence.

- - - - - - - - - - - - - KILLER MOVES - - - - - - - - - - - -

STOMP KICK

A "stomp kick" is a martial arts technique that involves the attacker raising his knee and then stomping on the victim—often while he's down. This can be done in an arcing axe motion or a direct straight stomp. Though it can be used as a technique to kick a standing victim, or even by someone on the floor kicking upward, it can be total murder when used to kick your opponent while they're down. Karate, kickboxing, Krav Maga, Kung Fu, and the U.S. Marines all teach the stomp kick as part of their fighting curriculum, although stomping on a fallen opponent's head is specifically banned by the UFC and other mixed martial arts organizations because of its potential to seriously injure or kill.

NINJA SWORD

The ninja were clans of hired assassins in feudal Japan, and their whole *raison d'être* was murder. What most people think of as a ninja sword, also known as a *Ninja-To*, is a straight-bladed sword with a wrapped handle and square *tsuba* (the part that separates the handle from the blade), as seen in hundreds of movies since the 1970s. The first Hollywood film to feature the Ninja-To was *Revenge of the Ninja*, staring Sho Kosugi in 1983, which helped popularize these swords worldwide despite some historical debate about whether or not these distinctive swords were truly used by the ninja back in the day. Unlike Samurai swords, which were intricately crafted by some of the world's best blade-smiths, ninja swords were typically not super well-made. The ninja had limited resources, so they just used what they had (or stole Samurai swords and then disappeared into thin air). Poof!

HEART ATTACK GUN

A "heart attack gun" sounds like something made up for a Barry Eisler novel or James Bond movie, but in fact it's a weapon that the United States government admitted to developing for the Central Intelligence Agency. This gun releases a small, poisonous dart into the victim's body. They might not feel anything, or might feel like they were bitten by an insect. The dart—which is actually composed of frozen poison—disintegrates immediately and releases a fatal chemical into the bloodstream that causes the victim to have a heart attack. The poison was engineered to be undetectable by modern forensic examination, so to any interested third party it would truly appear that the victim had a heart attack. The government's use of this weapon was made public during a hearing in 1975 outlining suspected rogue CIA activities.

- - - - - - - - - - - **FATAL FIREARMS** - - - - - - - - - - - -

BERETTA 9MM

Members of the armed forces in the United States are typically issued as a sidearm either the Beretta 9mm or the Colt 1911 .45. Beretta has been making guns since 1526. *Fifteen twenty six*! They weren't even called guns way back then; their product was at the time known as an "arquebus." In more recent years, the company's M9 pistol was adopted by the United States military. Durable and easy to maintain, the Beretta 9mm was deployed in Iraq, Afghanistan, and numerous other engagements. Given the 400+ years of manufacturing, many a man has met his maker at the business end of a Beretta firearm.

POP CULTURE **Beretta 9mm firearms have appeared in movies like *Minority Report* with Tom Cruise, *A Good Day to Die Hard* with Bruce Willis, and *Sharknado* with a bunch of flying killer sharks.**

- - - - - - - - - - - - **SNEAKY SABOTAGE** - - - - - - - - - - - -

DRUG OVERDOSE

From movies to mystery novels, murdering someone by injecting them with a lethal dose of an illegal narcotic, such as heroin, has become a well-worn trope that both eliminates the victim and disgraces them at the same time. But real-life murder via drug overdose doesn't have to be so hands on. In recent years, United States, prosecutors have begun charging drug dealers with murder should their customers die untimely deaths via overdose. And some would say it's a just response. In 2015, the Drug Enforcement Agency announced that drug overdoses caused twice as many deaths than firearms—46,000 deaths in 2013 alone.

POP CULTURE **Some conspiracy theorists suggest that the death of Marilyn Monroe was a murder staged to look like a drug overdose.**

- - - - - - - - - - - - - - THUG LIFE - - - - - - - - - - - - - - -

EXECUTION-STYLE SHOOTING

This dramatic method of murder involves killing someone at close range, typically by shooting victims in the back of the head while they are under strict controls such as tied by restraints or held by accomplices. Execution-style shootings are rampant in Mexico as a favored killing technique by the nation's many nefarious drug cartels. These are also known as "Chicago-style murders," because of the 1929 St. Valentines Day massacre, whereby six gangsters were killed execution-style. It's a popular misperception that "Chicago-style murder" involves pizza, roast beef, and hot dogs.

DEADLY DETAILS **Also qualifying as an execution-style shooting is the pre-planned and deliberate targeting and incapacitation of a specific vehicle, for the sole purpose of murdering the occupants.**

KUNG FU IRON PALM

The controversial art of kung fu's "iron palm" or "iron fist" training is said to be able to kill a man with a single slap. Through a combination of hand conditioning, power generation, anatomical knowledge, and precise control, the martial artist is meant to be able to "adjust" the damage his blow causes from merely crippling to, well, murderous. The legend of this almost supernatural skill is hundreds of years old, and proponents of it claim that the technique has been a carefully guarded secret in China until recent years. Some modern martial artists claiming to have this skill show their prowess by breaking boards and bricks—and should probably stick to inanimate objects, unless they want to wear the "iron bracelets" during arrest.

- - - - - - - - - - - **PERNICIOUS POISONS** - - - - - - - - - - -

CHRISTMAS PLANTS

Traditional Christmas decorations can be downright deadly— but probably not the ones you'd expect. Most people think poinsettias are very poisonous and can kill you if ingested. The truth is, even small children would have to eat several hundred poinsettia leaves to reach toxic levels (and they wouldn't, because the leaves taste awful). The pernicious plant to watch out for is holly and its pretty little toxic berries. Holly berries are bright red and look like the kind of thing you'd want to eat, but it doesn't take many to kill a small child or animal, and only a few more to get a full-size human into trouble.

POP CULTURE Halle Berry is also potentially murderous— at least in terms of killing you softly with her love.

81

AMANITA
MUSHROOMS

This exotic-looking mushroom is related to the lethal "Death Cap" mushroom (Page 103), but despite the Amanita muscaria's cute appearance in pop-culture everywhere from Super Mario Bros to generic lawn gnome ornaments, these red-capped mushrooms with little white knobblies are actually hallucinogenic toadstools. Not only do they contain a psychoactive agent called muscimol, but also they're quite poisonous. You won't just die—you'll first have visions of your boss dressed as a Little Bo Peep and riding a giant turtle while *Go Ask Alice* blares in the background. Ingesting too many can mean murder, since it only takes a little over a dozen of these mushrooms to kill a person.

SCYTHE

Often an icon of death itself, a scythe is an old-fashioned hand tool used to cut grass or crops. The Grim Reaper, a skeletal hooded figure that personifies Death, is often depicted carrying a scythe with which he "harvests" human souls. A long pole wielded with two hands, the scythe has a curved, single-edge blade jutting out from the handle and has been in use since ancient Rome, about 500 BC. And from then to now, the unstable have also used them as tools of murder. Many contemporary murders involving a scythe take place in the developing world, where the tool is still in relatively common farm use.

DEADLY DETAILS In the 1500s, a version of the scythe was designed specifically for military combat in Europe.

- - - - - - - - - MURDER MOST STRANGE - - - - - - - - -

BOWLING BALL

What a way to go! There are an estimated 6,000 bowling alleys in the United States alone, and with all of those bowlers there are bound to be some crazed players who just refuse to spare a life. Bowling balls weigh anywhere between eight and sixteen pounds, so when they're not on the lanes where they belong, they are completely capable of dealing a death strike. Case in point, a New Jersey man was killed at a Piscataway bowling alley when someone threw a bowling ball at his head during a late-night melee, and in the 2007 movie *There Will Be Blood*, actor Daniel Day-Lewis makes murderous use of an old-fashioned bowling pin—a fate surely better than putting on those rented shoes.

CAPOEIRA KICK

Capoeira is a Brazilian martial art that incorporates dance and acrobatics into its fighting curriculum, and dates back to when African slaves in Brazil would form a circle, disguising their fighting art as a dance. But just because these martial artists have sick dance skills doesn't mean that their art isn't killer. Capoeira really packs a punch, and is best known for its brutal spinning kicks, which put the whole body behind their impact. As recently as 2012, fighters have been killed by the powerful kicks of a capoeira practitioner.

DEADLY DETAILS **When pressed into actual combat, the art's flamboyantly acrobatic moves are sometimes jettisoned in favor of more direct and economical techniques.**

RADIOACTIVE ISOTOPES

Radioactive materials such as Cobalt-60, Iridium-192 and Caesium-137 are used with great caution and regulatory oversight in industrial and healthcare processes such as treating cancer patients or sterilizing foods in factories. But one of the scariest things about these potentially murderous materials is that these isotopes are not visible to the eye; you can't feel them or smell them or see them. Victims would not only fall ill to acute radiation syndrome, but also likely get some form of cancer. In an allegation of unthinkable obscenity, many East German citizens claim that the Stasi, the East German secret police, used either radioactive isotopes or X ray machines (or both) to induce cancer in political dissidents.

TRUE CRIME There's a lot of radioactive homicide in Russia; a former Presidential security officer, a truck driver, and the operator of a packing company were all intentionally murdered with radioactive material.

- - - - - - - - - - - - - - THUG LIFE - - - - - - - - - - - - - - -

BEATING

Beating another human being to death is one of the world's oldest forms of murder, and also one of its most obscene, given its up-close-and-personal nature. The earliest recorded instances of someone being beaten to death date back to ancient Egypt and beyond; many discoveries of human remains several thousands of years old show evidence of being beaten to death. During biblical times, the story of murderous brothers Cain and Abel illustrates one of the earliest such type of killing to become a widespread parable, and even in modern society, as shocking as it may seem, family and loved ones are still responsible for committing many of these gruesome murders.

- - - - - - - - - - - - FATAL FIREARMS - - - - - - - - - - - - -

SMITH & WESSON .38

At one time, the Smith & Wesson .38 was quite possibly the nation's most popular law enforcement revolver, especially when it came to its depiction in Hollywood: from film noir all the way up to contemporary cop flicks, police in *The Godfather*, *The Big Easy*, *Vertigo*, *In the Heat of the Night*, *Forced Vengeance*, *Beverly Hills*

Cop, *Lethal Weapon*, *Pulp Fiction*, *Starsky & Hutch*, and more all sported Smith & Wesson .38 revolvers. The gun has gone through a number of variations and models since the six-shooter first appeared in the nineteenth century—but with all of those guns in play, some of them were bound to wind up in the hands of a murderer.

---------- FATAL FIREARMS ----------

MAKAROV

The *Pistolet Makarova* is a Russian semi-automatic handgun that was commonly carried by police and military personnel of the Union of Soviet Socialist Republics (USSR) until the nation's collapse in 1991. And you can bet over its forty-something years of service, it's seen some murder. The gun was originally chambered in 9x18mm, and had an 8-round magazine capacity (new ones are a bit larger). While variants of the gun are still in production in China and Russia, they remain mostly collectors' pieces—especially those that actually saw service in the USSR and East Germany.

DEADLY DETAILS **The brainchild of brilliant engineer Nikolay Fyodorovich Makarov, the gun was selected as the result of a design contest and chosen to replace the popular Tokarev as the go-to service pistol.**

---------- SLASHER MADNESS ----------

BAYONET

A bayonet is a long, pointed blade that is fixed upon the end of a military rifle, turning the rifle into a short-range bladed weapon—a sort of makeshift spear. While not ideal, this gives the soldier at least a bit of range when entering a hand-to-hand engagement; and when not affixed to a rifle, the bayonet can serve as an all-purpose utility knife. Most armies in the world have issued bayonets to infantrymen throughout modern history, so there are a lot of them about. And they're perfectly legal to own, though apparently not everyone can be trusted with one. In 2008, a UK man stabbed his neighbor to death with a bayonet because he claimed the neighbor's music was too loud.

- - - - - - - - - - - - - - - THUG LIFE - - - - - - - - - - - - - - -

DRAGGING (BEHIND CAR/HORSE)

What an especially awful way to go. From horse-drawn carriages to today's modern motorcars, it seems like some people can't help but use transportation as a deadly weapon. In 2013, a 61-year-old Florida woman was arrested for dragging her ex-husband behind a pickup truck because she was jealous of him bringing another woman to her house. She allegedly shocked the man with a cattle prod, then beat him with the help of two friends before the trio tied him up and dragged him half a mile down the road. While the group was looking for a place to bury the body, the poor guy jumped out of the truck bed and ran to a nearby house for help. Seeing a marriage fail so badly is always a drag.

DEADLY DETAILS Some people do this to themselves on purpose for kicks by "skitching"—being pulled behind a car on a skateboard, rollerblades or inner-tube. You pays your money and you takes your chances.

THIRST

Holding people prisoner and denying them water is as murderous as putting a gun to their heads. Human beings need a LOT of water to stay alive and healthy. It typically takes between seven and fourteen days to die of hunger, but depending on the individual, the environment, and the level of activity involved, people can die of thirst in as quickly as three days. (According to the *Guinness Book of World Records*, the longest anyone has gone without food or water and survived was eighteen days.) Water helps your body regulate its temperature, flushes out toxins, carries nutrients, and oxygen to cells and helps keep your eyes, mouth, and other wet bits as they should be. Without it, let's just say bad things happen.

NINJA THROWING SPIKE

Included in the ninja's arsenal of weapons disguised as everyday items such as chopsticks or hairpins, ninja throwing spikes look like long, well-balanced knitting needles and are another form of *shuriken* or thrown, sharp weapon. While it's possible to kill somebody with a throwing spike (you see it in ninja movies all the time), they were primarily used by the ninja to distract their opponents while preparing to mount their primary attack via a sword or other more serious weapon. Also potentially dangerous is the bro-tastic Spike TV network, which can kill hours of otherwise productive time via UFC fight reruns.

MERCURY

Much like the band Pantera, mercury is a heavy metal that just isn't good for you in large quantities. Mercury occurs in many states—and any of them can kill you deader than a box of rocks. It's a super-handy element, used in medicine and lab work; most people are familiar with mercury in a thermometer. But direct contact will blast your kidneys, hurt your lungs, damage your brain, or give you a bunch of creepy diseases. One of the most notorious mercury-fueled murders occurred in 1898 when a wealthy but twisted playboy began poisoning people he didn't like with mercury cyanide, including a man who'd defeated him in a weightlifting contest at the Knickerbocker Athletic Club in New York. Talk about being mad as a hatter.

CZ 75

The CZ 75 is a semi-automatic handgun from the Czech Republic, manufactured by *Ceska zbrojovka* specifically for the export market. While most of these guns are used for fighting crimes, not committing them—they're used as law enforcement service pistols in places like Brazil, Egypt, Poland, Russia, Thailand, and Turkey—over a million of the guns have been made since their introduction in 1976. So at least one of them is bound to have been held in the hands of a murderer. Fired in either single-action or double-action mode, CZ 75 pistols share many design characteristics with the Browning Hi-Power pistol and have either a 12- or 26-round magazine capacity depending on the model. That's a lot of potential murder!

PIZZA CUTTER

I t's entirely possible to kill someone using a pizza cutter—and not just with high cholesterol. The utility in a pizza cutter is the wheel-like blade, which cuts continuously with applied pressure. And it doesn't care whether you're cutting through people or pepperoni. Indeed, even the Transportation Safety Administration (TSA) has recognized the deadly potential of the pizza cutter as a weapon and seized them from would-be passengers trying to travel by the slice. In 2008, a horrific murder in Iowa listed a pizza cutter among its deadly murder weapons. And in 2015, two twenty-something brothers in Oslo, Norway murdered a man with a pizza cutter because he owed them money.

DEADLY DETAILS **Delivering pizza in the United States is a dangerous undertaking! In 2014 alone, at least twenty pizza delivery drivers were shot. They're an attractive target for the unscrupulous when you think about it: carrying food and cash, and generally unable to carry a weapon due to company policies.**

- - - - - - - - - **MURDER MOST STRANGE** - - - - - - - - -

JAVELIN

T hese days known primarily as a track and field or Olympic event, a javelin is a light spear originally designed to be thrown in combat. The use of the throwing stick dates back to the Paleolithic era, and most cultures developed some form of this weapon at some point in the past. Along with this widespread use, came its inevitable employment against one's own countrymen in a flash of hot temper. Though not an intentional murder but a terrible accident, in 2012 a German referee at a javelin-throwing event was speared through the throat by an errant hurl, and subsequently died from his injuries.

- - - - - - - - - - - - - **KILLER MOVES** - - - - - - - - - - - - -

KUNG FU KWAN DAO

A kwan dao is basically a sword-on-a-stick, and if you get stuck with one, consider yourself murdered. The kwan dao (also spelled *guandao*) dates back to around the year 200 AD in China, and is the brainchild of General Guan Yu, the weapon's namesake. It was adopted by martial artists in ancient China, and used at the Shaolin temple—slicing armor like a rice bun. Today, traditional Chinese martial artists use the kwan dao as a part of their weapons curriculum, as do contemporary "wushu" stage performers. It's hard to turn on a kung fu movie—either from the 1970s or one of today's modern tales—without seeing one in use by a shaven-headed warrior monk.

- - - - - - - - - - - - **SNEAKY SABOTAGE** - - - - - - - - - - - -

MISSING SIGNAGE

S ign theft is remarkably common. Injuries or deaths can occur when roadway signs, stop signs in particular, are stolen. Although the sign thieves are typically charged with manslaughter rather than murder (since the tragic outcomes are usually more the result of stupidity than malice), someone with more nefarious plans could cause an intentional death by removing a roadway sign declaring "Bridge Out" or some other critical communication that would result in a potentially life-threatening driving situation. The same holds true for signage around dangerous terrain such as a challenging ski slope. Removing really important signs such as "Danger, Cliff!" or "Caution! Extreme Terrain," or "Do Not Leave the Run: Crevasses!" could be potentially fatal.

TRUE CRIME So many signs are stolen on Route 66 that it's often difficult to know when you're actually on the road, and so many Abbey Road signs were stolen in London that the city had to permanently affix them on buildings.

- - - - - - - - - - PERNICIOUS POISONS - - - - - - - - - -

S*A*RIN

This colorless, odorless organophosphorus compound comes in liquid form—and can kill you deader than a doornail. Even in low doses, breathing in sarin fumes paralyzes the victim's lung muscles—resulting in death in as quickly as one minute after exposure. The most infamous civilian use of sarin was the 1995 mass murder of thirteen people in Tokyo, Japan by a religious fanatic who released sarin gas into the Tokyo subway. Almost 6,000 people experienced difficulty breathing, bleeding, fatigue, vision problems, and other symptoms as a result of the attack. Eye witnesses described the scene as looking like a battlefield. The majority of victims say they still experience fatigue and vision problems to this day. The United States government stopped making this deadly nerve gas in the 1950s, and it's been classified a weapon of mass destruction by the United Nations, so making it is outlawed no matter who you are.

SCALPING

S calping is the brutal act of murdering someone by cutting off the top of his head as a trophy (or removing the scalp of an already dead person). Most people associate the practice of scalping with the frontier skirmishes between European settlers and Native Americans in North America, but it wasn't only one-way traffic—some Mexican and American governments also paid citizens a bounty for the scalps of Native American warriors. Cormac McCarthy's dark novel *Blood Meridian* details one such grim expedition. Modern drug cartels have also been known to employ this method of murder. In 2012, a Native American woman was found scalped to death in rural Kentucky; police are still working the case.

DEADLY DETAILS **Though popular culture depicts scalping as a Native American practice, this ritual can be traced back at least as far back as 440 BC, to the ancient Eurasian society of Scythia.**

- - - - - - - - - - - - **FATAL FIREARMS** - - - - - - - - - - - -

MOSIN NAGANT

T his deadly firearm holds twice the murderous potential of most military rifles, because if you don't feel like firing it, you could always club someone over the head with the unwieldy thing. Designed by Russian Imperial Army Captain Sergei Mosin and Belgian gun designer Leon Nagant, this big and heavy 7.62-caliber military rifle was issued to Russian troops in 1891. Eight out of ten Germans in World War II were killed with this gun. And thirty-seven MILLION have been made in Russia since its creation, not to mention a number of knock-offs from places like China. That's why you can buy one still today at almost any American gun show nationwide for only a few hundred bucks. You can see stars toting Mosin Nagants in Hollywood action flicks such as *The Good German, Enemy at the Gates,* and the modern remake of *Flight of the Phoenix.*

POWER TOOLS

L ike almost any other man-made implement, today's modern power tools can be used to build a better life—or take one away. Plenty of people hurt themselves without any help (emergency rooms see around 37,000 folks each year who have been using power nailers, for example). But in addition to these risks, power saws, drills, nail guns, and more have all been used by the mentally unsound to help usher the unfortunate and unsuspecting into the afterlife.

TRUE CRIME **In one especially grisly instance, a murder victim in Sydney, Australia was shot thirty-four times in the head with a gas-fired nail gun. Police even released x-rays of the victim's skull in an appeal to generate leads, but the murder still remains unsolved.**

- - - - - - - - - - - SLASHER MADNESS - - - - - - - - - - -

SCISSORS

Y our average, everyday pair of scissors have played a role in a surprising number of murders, likely due to the fact that almost every household has a pair. The earliest known pair of scissors was found in Mesopotamia around 3,500 years ago, and ever since, their darkest and most desperate users have been tempted to use them to cut someone down. The news is rife with heat-of-the-moment murder-by-scissors: in Japan, more citizens were killed in 2011 with scissors than guns. In Britain, a woman murdered her husband in 2012 with a pair of scissors because he refused to help her clean the house. Shear madness, I tell you.

- - - - - - - - - - **PERNICIOUS POISONS** - - - - - - - - - -

EYE DROPS

In 2012, a 33-year-old woman admitted to poisoning her boyfriend with Visine over a period of three years. Visine is that magical eye drop that turns bloodshot late-night-happy-hour eyes into clear, responsible went-to-bed-early eyes. Clearly not using the product as directed, the woman poured copious amounts of the stuff into her boyfriend's drinks around a dozen times. With an active ingredient called tetrahydrozoline, products like this are vassal constrictors that shrink the blood vessels—and this stunt could have killed the poor guy. Ingesting too much tetrahydrozoline will in extreme cases give you blurred vision, nervousness, nausea, blue fingernails, seizures, and eventually death.

- - - - - - - - - - - **SNEAKY SABOTAGE** - - - - - - - - - - -

TROPICAL DISEASE

There are thousands of diseases known to man, some common and others quite rare. It's possible to murder someone by intentionally exposing them to a disease that's little known in the developed world—throwing off attending physicians until it's just too late for the unfortunate victim. Many tropical diseases are spread by mosquitos, which according to the World Health Organization are the deadliest animals in the world (deadlier than snakes, sharks, or the turducken). Malaria kills more than 600,000 people every year. Real-life tales of intentional murder-by-tropical-disease allude researchers. But, then again, how would we know?

POP CULTURE In one of Sir Arthur Conan Doyle's Sherlock Holmes stories, *The Dying Detective*, the author used an ambiguous tropical disease (perhaps melioidosis, found in contaminated water in parts of Southeast Asia) as a murder weapon.

- - - - - - - - - - - - KILLER MOVES - - - - - - - - - - - -

FENCING FOIL

A fencing "foil" is the technical term for the thin pointy sword with a rounded guard used in the sport of fencing. And it's no stranger to murder, given the age and popularity of fencing worldwide over the years. The foil dates back to France in the 1700s, when it was used to train gentlemen on how to handle their swords (back then, gentlemen carried swords rather than smart phones). In those days, dueling to the death was common, so working with the fencing foil was meant to ensure that you could protect your honor without getting skewered. Fencing has been an Olympic sport since 1896, so watch your back…er…your front…next time you're at The Games. En garde!

POP CULTURE In *Over My Dead Body* by Rex Stout, Nero Wolfe investigates a murder-by-foil at a fencing club.

CHAINSAW

The terrible thing about a chainsaw is that it doesn't know the difference between cutting through pine trees or people. Because of their efficient and terrifying nature, chainsaws have been used in a number of murders in the developed world. They're especially popular with members of the Mexican drug cartels, whose

gruesome murder methods often double as attempts to intimidate citizens, public officials, and the media. Pop-culture did its part too: the 1974 horror film *The Texas Chainsaw Massacre* (*not* actually based on a true story, despite original marketing), the 1983 Oliver Stone movie *Scarface*, and the television show *Dexter* all helped put the fear of chainsaw murder into the public's imagination.

TOKAREV TT

The Tokarev is a semi-automatic pistol made in Russia and used by Russia's military and law enforcement communities from around 1930 to the present day in places like North Korea and Pakistan. Over 1.7 million have been made to date. Designed by Fedor Tokarev, this 7.62-caliber pistol has an 8-round capacity and enough recoil to shake a Rolex watch clean off of your wrist. Because they're cheap and easy to find, these guns are common "throw down" weapons for criminals.

POP CULTURE **When you see a movie with Soviet-era soldiers or police, they are almost always toting Tokarevs. The pistol has appeared in the original *Red Dawn*, *Gorky Park*, *The Pianist*, *American Beauty*, *The Usual Suspects*, and *Blackhawk Down*—as well as the James Bond films *Octopussy* and *For Your Eyes Only*.**

REMOTE-CONTROL DRONES

Remote-controlled drones are used to deliver packages, conduct surveillance, fight fires, manage agriculture, and other harmless ventures. You can actually build or buy these drones for very little money. But, of course, they can also be used to kill. The United States military uses drones to conduct operations around the world simultaneously—and many missions are of the deadly variety. This controversial combination of remote-control aircraft and deadly capabilities is creating a radical shift in the way warfare and domestic law enforcement—and potentially murder—are conducted. It seems like only a matter of time before private citizens raised on video games decide to employ these high-tech machines to commit murder IRL.

GUT SHOT

As the name implies, to "gut-shoot" someone means shooting the poor victim in the stomach and then waiting for him or her to bleed to death slowly. While getting shot in the stomach doesn't automatically mean death, the clock is ticking. Even if the victim receives immediate medical attention and doesn't bleed to death, the risk of fatal infection from a stomach wound is high, given the acids and bacteria in that part of your body. It is a painful way to die, and an especially cruel way to murder someone.

DEADLY DETAILS When hunters go after deer or other game animals, they go out of their way to avoid gut-shooting so the animal doesn't suffer.

- - - - - - - - - - - - SNEAKY SABOTAGE - - - - - - - - - - - -

DROWNING IN THE TUB

A nice bath is meant to be a place to relax and forget about your troubles; to unwind and scrub away the stress of the day. And often, it's a place where couples kick back in the candlelight—a popular romantic scene you'll find in books and movies and on TV. But it can also be a crime scene. Forcing someone's head underwater is a gruesome and intimate means of murder. Typically, when you hear about someone having been drowned in the bathtub, the victim and perpetrator are related or romantically involved, as in the 2000 thriller *What Lies Beneath*, where Harrison Ford's character tries to drown his wife in the tub after administering a paralyzing drug. So if you have any reason to doubt your beloved's intentions, it may be best to just take a shower.

DEADLY DETAILS **Popcorn magnate Orville Redenbacher died in a whirlpool bathtub, though it wasn't murder—he popped off naturally of a heart attack at the seasoned age of 88.**

- - - - - - - - - - - - - KILLER MOVES - - - - - - - - - - - - -

LONG STAFF

A long staff is a traditional martial arts weapon consisting of an approximately six-foot-long pole made from wax wood (derived from the Chinese privet tree), oak, rattan, or some other durable material, and it can be used to block, strike, sweep, poke, push, and disarm opponents. The long staff is one of the traditional kung fu weapons first trained by warrior monks at the Shaolin temple. It was a versatile weapon back in the days when one depended on fighting skills to survive attacks from bandits and such—its length gave the defender range. The exact height of the staff varies by art and practitioner, but they're all capable of killing via blunt force trauma to the head. Later in history, Japanese martial artists also adopted the long staff. Even the ninja employed it in their deadly art. Kung fu movies from the 1970s often depict monks and masters killing their foes with the simple staff.

DEATH CAP MUSHROOMS

Amanita phalloides, also known as the "Death Cap" Mushroom, is a greenish grey basidiomycete fungus shaped like an umbrella. They contain Amatoxin—a deadly compound found in a number of wild mushrooms including not just the Death Cap but also the Amanita mushroom (Page 82). Unlike the bright-red Amanita, the Death Cap is additionally dangerous because it looks like so many other benign non-toxic 'shrooms you put on your pizza or salad. But eat one of these bad boys, and you'll be throwing up and cramping within a few hours. If not treated, you're looking at total liver failure and death!

TRUE CRIME The Holy Roman Emperor Charles VI is said to have been murdered by the poison of a Death Cap Mushroom.

CAT O' NINE TAILS

The cat o' nine tails is a wicked little rope whip with nine smaller whips or "tails" at the end. The ends of each smaller tail are either frayed into even smaller pieces or tied into knots to maximize the pain. Killing someone with a cat o' nine tails is not just murder, but torture as well. In fact, this cruel weapon was initially designed specifically as a tool of torture. The British Navy used them to enforce courts martial, and they were used in British prisons well into the twentieth century, and in Australia as late as 1957. A few hundred lashes with a cat o'nine tails could kill a man, and many met their end this way. In 1846, a British soldier from London died after being sentenced to 150 lashes with the cat o'nine tails, starting a movement to ban the use of such lashings. Great Britain finally banned its use in 1948.

DEADLY DETAILS In Trinidad and Tobago, they still use "the cat" as a means of corporal punishment. It's restricted to use on males only, and only those older than 18 years of age. Nope, still doesn't seem humane.

- - - - - - - - - - - - - THUG LIFE - - - - - - - - - - - - -

BOOBY TRAP

The idea of a homemade device triggered by an unsuspecting victim is generally known as the prevue of guerilla warfare, or annoying older brothers. A booby trap can be simple or complicated, but while they're occasionally meant more to surprise than to injure, they can also be seriously deadly. During WWII, the Nazis booby-trapped everything from helmets lying on the ground to houses to rifles leaning against buildings. They even booby-trapped chocolate bars. (Not the chocolate!) The Vietcong in Vietnam would rig their flags so that when an enemy overtook their position and went to pull their flag down, a hand grenade was detonated. In most countries, it's illegal to set up a booby trap at your house for security purposes (or for murder, for that matter).

DEADLY DETAILS The word "booby" in this context comes from the Spanish word *bobo*, which means someone not too smart.

QUICKSAND

Quicksand is a liquefied soil composed of stuff like clay and sand mixed into some sort of water source. It looks solid, but if you step on it, you'll sink and the solid particulates will re-form around you—taking lots of force to re-liquefy. You're more likely to simply get stuck in it than be killed, though if you keep struggling, you can certainly drown or become immobilized long enough to succumb to your environment. Just recently, an unfortunate lady in Antigua drowned in quicksand. But in works of fiction, people are murdered by getting thrown or tricked into quicksand left and right, from Sherlock Holmes stories to soap operas. Theories that most of the world's quicksand actually exists on the set of *Gilligan's Island* have not been substantiated.

COLT PYTHON

This once popular revolver is a .357 Magnum made by Colt's Manufacturing Company in Connecticut. And it packs a murderous punch. Double-action and with a six-round cylinder, it was introduced in the 1950s and discontinued in 1999—citing, among other reasons, the mounting costs of lawsuits against it—but during its time, it made a big impact. Available in a shiny nickel finish or a dark royal blue, these guns could even be equipped with a scope and used to hunt. The gun's intimidating look made it a Hollywood favorite, appearing in everything from *Scarface* to *Silence of the Lambs*, and Laurence Fishburne even packed a Colt Python in *Boyz n the Hood*.

- - - - - - - - - - - - KILLER MOVES - - - - - - - - - - - - -

MANRIKI GUSARI

This traditional Japanese martial arts weapon is composed of a chain with a small iron weight at each end. It was useful in situations where the martial artist could not carry a sword and needed a weapon that was easily concealable. The weapon was adopted by the ninja in ancient Japan, but also used by police in those days as a typically non-lethal alternative to the sword. But it's totally possible to kill someone with a manriki gusari via blunt force strike to the head or strangulation. Of course, it takes training to use a manriki gusari effectively—otherwise you just might end up murdering yourself.

PAPER CUTTER

Yep, seriously. People have been killed all over the world using the humble office or school paper cutter. It's not the first thing you'd think of when someone says "murder weapon." But, then again, murderers aren't always known for their thinking skills. A paper cutter sits on a desktop, with a square base and a long handled straight blade that raises and lowers like a slot machine handle. While unwieldy and awkward, these things do have razor-sharp, 24-inch long (or even longer) blades. Just a friendly reminder not to make anyone mad at the office.

ALLERGIC REACTIONS

People can have deadly anaphylactic reactions to a large number of things, including foods, drugs, or insect bites. While typically treatable, not getting prompt or appropriate treatment can be life-threatening. According to *Science Daily*, you are statistically more likely to be murdered than you are to die of a food allergy. But what if it's both? It's entirely possible to murder someone with severe allergies by intentionally exposing them to food they can't have (such as shellfish for some) or reaction-causing stinging and biting creatures. In the movies, murderers engineer deadly allergies all the time. In real life, most people brought up on charges of murder via promoting an allergic reaction did so by mistake. A pair of British restaurant workers, for example, were arrested after a patron died from eating curry that contained peanuts.

GOLF CLUB

Fore! Every year, golfers wig out and use their nine irons to hit new lows for humanity. Golf clubs make for common murder weapons because they're handy, discreet, and high-impact. A good golfer can hit a golf ball with the hard head of a club at 180 miles per hour—more than twice the speed of hurricane force winds—and it only takes a few pounds of pressure, and a little bad luck, to die from a head wound. Surprisingly, if you've ever tried golf, most of this murderous rage doesn't actually occur on the golf course.

HEDGE TRIMMERS

Hedge trimmers come in two varieties: the manual type, which look like large scissors, and the electric variety, which look like a small, flat chainsaw. While neither may seem very deadly, both types have been used in either murder or to seriously injure someone. In 2013, a clinically depressed woman lugged electric hedge clippers (orange extension cord and all) into her nine-year-old daughter's bedroom and tried to kill her, though luckily, the husband was able to save the girl. Sounds like a great excuse if there ever was one to hire out all of your lawn work.

POP CULTURE   In the campy 1981 horror flick *The Burning*, a psycho kills an entire raft of campers with a pair of scissor-like hedge clippers (not pretty).

- - - - - - - - - MURDER MOST STRANGE - - - - - - - - -

CURSES AND MAGIC SPELLS

Actual science may not back up the existence of curses and magic spells, but that doesn't stop some people from believing that you can kill someone by putting a curse on them, or by using some kind of black magic. Grigori Rasputin, a Russian royal advisor who also fancied himself a magician and mystic, cursed the aristocratic Romanov family in 1916, saying that they would be dead in a year. Indeed, the Romanovs—the Tsar, his family, and associates—were shortly thereafter all murdered by rebels. Just a coincidence? Maybe. But if you know someone who purports to have the power to curse, best get on their good side just in case.

DEADLY DETAILS   In some African countries, you can still be put on trial for witchcraft.

- - - - - - - - - - - FATAL FIREARMS - - - - - - - - - - -

RUGER 10/22

The Ruger 10/22 is a semi-automatic rifle chambered in .22LR caliber ammunition and carrying a 10-round magazine capacity. First made in 1964, the 10/22 was an instant hit with ranchers, hunters, and people who just wanted to shoot a gun that fired inexpensive rounds at beer bottles and whatnot. Most .22 rifles were made for kids at the time; considered a "starter rifle" until they came of age to get a "real" hunting rifle. But the Ruger 10/22 was a quality gun made for adults—cheap to buy and shoot. While many dismiss .22LR as a less-than-lethal round, those people are wrong. In 2012, a Staten Island man known as the "Son of Sal" was charged with murdering three Brooklyn storekeepers with a Ruger 10/22.

- - - - - - - - - - - - KILLER MOVES - - - - - - - - - - - -

ROPE DART

This traditional Chinese martial arts weapon is exactly what it says—a metal dart on the end of an about ten-foot piece of rope. And it's completely capable of kung fu style murder via blunt force trauma to the head. Fighters who have trained with the rope dart can gain a significant reach advantage over their opponents— striking and entangling their enemies in a variety of crafty ways. It takes a lot of training to fight with one of these, and you often see rope dart practitioners wowing the crowds at kung fu demonstrations with their skill and acrobatics. They've even made their way into murderous video games such as *Assassin's Creed*.

AIR EMBOLISM

Technically known as a gas or air embolism, this medical condition occurs by introducing air into the vascular system—most commonly through an intravenous line used during routine hospital treatments. If a large gas bubble (about 200 cc) gets caught in the heart, it can stop the flow of blood and lead to death. There have been a number of cases whereby not-very-sane nurses have murdered their helpless patients intentionally in this manner. Of course, this also happens unintentionally when nurses, paramedics, or phlebotomists don't use proper technical protocols in treating patients. So deadly is this situation that it was once used as a method of euthanasia in Germany.

SCREWDRIVER

This useful tool dates back to the Middle Ages…and has also been the means of many a murder, largely due to the sheer massive number of them out in the world. To murder someone with a screwdriver, you've gotta skewer them like a kabob—and sometimes one wound alone could do the deadly trick. Screwdrivers can also be sharpened to make them that much more deadly, but even straight off the shelf, they're something to watch out for. In 2013, a husband in LA stabbed his wife in the face with a screwdriver; he was angry that she hadn't bought him a Valentine's Day present. (We see why; he's just not that sweet.) Just recently, a Denver man riding in a Cadillac Escalade was stabbed sixty-four times with a screwdriver by someone in the backseat. The victim died, and the perpetrator was sentenced to life in prison.

- - - - - - - - - - - **FATAL FIREARMS** - - - - - - - - - - -

SKS

The Soviet-made SKS military carbine can dish out a lot of murder—in not very much time. This 7.62-caliber semi-automatic long gun holds ten rounds in a stripper clip (a metal speed-loader that holds several rounds); it's good up to about 400 meters with a competent operator. The SKS was designed by weapons specialist Sergei Gavrilovich Simonov to fill a need for shorter-range fire fights without struggling to use huge, heavy weapons like the barely luggable Mosin-Nagant. In 2004, a man armed with an SKS rifle went crazy and killed eight deer hunters in the woods after he was caught hunting illegally on the victims' land.

- - - - - - - - - - - **SNEAKY SABOTAGE** - - - - - - - - - - -

PILLOWS

Meant to provide comfort, pillows can also provide sickos with a murder weapon. This typically happens when the killer uses a pillow to cover the mouth and nose of a victim (often sleeping) until he or she can no longer breathe. The Roman emperor Tiberius is said to have died from having been smothered by a pillow—no sleep has been safe since. In 2010, an Australian man smothered his wife with a pillow for refusing to have sex with him. In the 2007 film *Before the Devil Knows You're Dead*, Philip Seymour Hoffman played a son smothered to death by his father for having staged a robbery that led to a murder! Sleep tight.

- - - - - - - - - - - - - **KILLER MOVES** - - - - - - - - - - - - - -

JIU JITSU THROW

The traditional Japanese martial art of Jiu Jitsu (which translates into something like "soft or flexible art or technique") teaches practitioners how to throw, hold, and grapple opponents—and its fighters are especially good at fighting on the ground. But among its many potentially deadly techniques are its throws: hip throws, shoulder throws, ankle throws, scissor throws, head throws, and neck throws. Any one of these throws could smack a man's head upon the pavement with deadly results.

POP CULTURE   Rapper Ice T, director Guy Ritchie, actor Ed O'Neill (of *Married with Children* and *Modern Family* fame), Russian president Vladimir Putin, and German chancellor Angela Merkel have all either studied Jiu Jitsu or its cousin, Judo.

- - - - - - - - - - - **PERNICIOUS POISONS** - - - - - - - - - - - -

ACONITE

Aconite is a toxin produced by a plant known as *aconitum monkshood*, which grows well in some mountainous areas. Aconitum flowers can be white, purple, yellow, or pink, and look like little helmets, hence its nickname "devil's helmet." It's also known as "wolfsbane" because its poison was once used to kill wolves. Consuming a few dozen milliliters of this flower's toxin will kill a person deader than a dumbbell in just a few hours. First the victims will be sick to their stomachs. Then they'll become numb. When severe cardiovascular issues ensue, they'll feel nothing at all. The key to fighting the aconite toxin is knowing what you're dealing with; in 2014 a gardener working on a British millionaire's estate touched aconite flowers and died of multiple organ failure just days later. Nobody figured out the culprit until it was too late.

TRUE CRIME **Cleopatra was said to have been poisoned with a combination of aconite, hemlock, and opium.**

- - - - - - - - - - - FATAL FIREARMS - - - - - - - - - - -

THE REMINGTON 700

I t's one of the most successful and flexible bolt-action rifles in production, and is popular with both hunters and law enforcement officers. And, potentially, murderers as well. Available in a variety of calibers, Remington Arms first started selling these guns in the early 1960s. Immediately popular with deer hunters, these inexpensive and simple rifles proliferated around the country. Dozens of variants were produced, and both the police and military not just in the United States but also in places like Canada, Malaysia, and the Philippines began relying on this solid long gun. This thing is straight out of a Bambi nightmare!

POP CULTURE **This gun is old school country boy; Josh Brolin sports one in _No Country for Old Men_, and it pops up in the hands of multiple people on the Wyoming-based TV crime series _Longmire_.**

HUNTING ACCIDENT

I t's a tragic situation known worldwide: two individuals go out hunting, but only one comes back. It has all the elements for danger: deadly weapons, remote locations, and nobody else around to dispute what REALLY happened. While people are mistaken for game and accidentally shot almost every year, sometimes it's not really an accident at all. Humans have long lured their prey into the dark and deadly woods. In 1995, one Colorado woman led her husband into the beautiful mountain wilderness for a day of deer hunting—then had her ex-husband shoot him with a stolen .308-caliber rifle. Investigators became suspicious when they realized the man had been shot three times.

TRUE CRIME **Unpopular King William II of England was shot with an arrow under mysterious circumstances while out hunting in 1100.**

- - - - - - - - - MURDER MOST STRANGE - - - - - - - - -

SPEAR GUN

A spear gun is a rifle-looking device that projects a metal spear, used to spear fish underwater. It's a bit like a crossbow, though the mechanical force of the gun is produced either by a strong rubber band or highly compressed air. Chances are, the only time you've ever actually seen a spear gun is in the movies. But in recent years, more murders have been committed via spear gun than one might think—though not as many as you see in James Bond flicks. A soggy 007 has come up against spear guns in *License to Kill*, *Tomorrow Never Dies*, *The Spy Who Loved Me*, and *Thunderball*.

TOMAHAWK

A tomahawk is a small, straight hatchet historically used by Native Americans. The name comes from the Powhatan word *tamahaac*. Originally, their blades were made of sharpened stone or deer horn. But after contact with European settlers, iron-making and bartering made possible the implementation of steel tomahawk heads. Both natives and settlers depended on these useful tools not only for hand-to-hand combat, but also for everyday working. Early North American newspapers were filled with stories of tomahawk murders, but nowadays they're sold as novelties, used for camping, or thrown in competitions.

DEADLY DETAILS Some Native Americans would drill a hole through the tomahawk shaft and fashion a bowl into the back of the blade head, allowing them to smoke tobacco through their tomahawks.

- - - - - - - - - - - - - **KILLER MOVES** - - - - - - - - - - - - - -

WALKING CANE

A stick that can be used to help the elderly or the infirm get around a bit easier is almost as old as mankind itself. In eighteenth-century Europe, fashion dictated that a gentleman always carry a walking cane, whether or not their physiology demanded one. In Robert Louis Stevenson's famous story, *The Strange Case of Dr. Jekyll and Mr. Hyde*, the "evil" side of the story's subject comes out when he murders a Member of Parliament with a cane—something even mentally balanced Britons have a longing to do on occasion. The beauty of such a weapon is that it's always with you…but if you can't control yourself, it's probably best to leave it at home in lieu of something less deadly.

THALLIUM

Thallium is a chemical rarely found in nature; it's a byproduct produced during refining of heavy metal sulfide ores, such as zinc or lead. Thallium serves a number of legitimate commercial uses, mostly in the field of electronics and industrial manufacturing, but even touching this metal with your bare hands can be lethal, so it's used modestly. The soft, gray metal is so toxic that it was once used in rat poison and other pesticides, but is now banned given the serious health risks occurring from exposure.

TRUE CRIME In the 1950s, thallium's popularity as a rat poison in Australia led to numerous people being poisoned. The 2011 documentary, *Recipe for Murder*, explored the craze.

- - - - - - - - - MURDER MOST STRANGE - - - - - - - - -

SUPER-LOUD STEREO

British singer and songwriter Ed Sheeran once said that if he ever died of a heart attack, he'd want it to be because he was playing his stereo too loud. And some experts say that it's totally possible to be killed—or to kill someone—via a super-loud blast of bass, though the circumstances would have to be just right. For instance, if the victim has an underlying heart condition, such as something called Long QT Syndrome, it's very possible to cause potentially deadly heart irregularities by playing loud music (it's more the resulting excitement rather than the noise itself). Of course, you're also a potential murder *victim* yourself if you're the one playing loud music inconsiderately. In 2014, a man at a convenience store opened fire on a group of teenagers because he thought their music was too loud. One of the teens died, and the shooter went to prison.

- - - - - - - - - - - FATAL FIREARMS - - - - - - - - - - -

SAVAGE 99

The Savage Model 99 is a popular lever-action rifle first introduced in the United States in 1899. Arthur Savage was a Jamaican New Yorker, and his rifle was immediately popular as a solid and inexpensive tool for hunting and home defense. Chambered in a number of hunter-friendly rounds, such as .30-.30 Winchester, the rifle had a nice, flat trajectory. Original models used a rotary magazine, but later models had a conventional box cartridge. They were produced for more than seventy-five years until 1984, which means a lot of potential murder. But their popularity as a sporting rifle continues; you still see hunters using them from time to time.

DEADLY DETAILS Later in life, Mr. Savage went on to own the largest ranch in Australia!

- - - - - - - - - - - SLASHER MADNESS - - - - - - - - - - -

HALBERD

Also known as a Swiss voulge, a halberd is a long and pointed spear with an axe blade mounted a foot or so from the spear's tip. Dating back to the fourteenth century, these weapons were popular for use on horseback, and fighters skilled with halberds were known as halberdiers. The Swiss Guard, who protect the Vatican, still use halberds as their unit's ceremonial weapons. (They also, in case of an actual Papal smack-down, carry Sig 552 Commando model submachine guns—so don't make fun of their clowny-looking trousers.)

TRUE CRIME It's been said that the apostle Matthew, the Duke of Burgundy, and King Richard III were all killed by halberds in battle.

- - - - - - - - - - - - - - - THUG LIFE - - - - - - - - - - - - - - -

"BLANKET PARTY"

A "blanket party" is a type of hazing or corporal punishment administered by peers in the middle of the night (such as at an army barracks by fellow soldiers). Typically, the aim is not murderous, but still rather violent and intended to motivate the victim into changing his or her behavior in some way without having to involve superior officers. Blanket parties have been seen on screen in military thrillers such as *Full Metal Jacket*, where an underperforming Marine Corps recruit is beaten in his bunk, and in *A Few Good Men*, where a struggling Marine at Guantanamo Bay is accidentally killed during such an incident, leading to the prosecution of the facility's senior officers by Tom Cruise and his inherent awesomeness.

- - - - - - - - - - - - SNEAKY SABOTAGE - - - - - - - - - - - -

SKYDIVING ACCIDENT

Believe it or not, skydivers actually do want to live through the experience. It's just that sometimes their skydiving companions might have other, less noble, ideas about the jump. Murdering a skydiver by tampering with their gear or otherwise sabotaging the dive has happened a number of times around the world. In Belgium in 2010, a schoolteacher was found guilty of sabotaging another woman's skydiving parachute because they were both in love with the same man. All three involved in the love triangle were skydivers, and she actually cut her rival's parachute cords prior to the jump then watched her fall from the plane. But while you can make somebody fall from you, you can't make somebody fall for you. The murderer went down for the crime, no doubt lonelier than ever.

- - - - - - - - - - **PERNICIOUS POISONS** - - - - - - - - - - -

WARFARIN

Warfarin is a popular medication (also sold under the brand name Coumadin) that saves lives every year by helping prevent blood clots. But like any other prescription, it's a potential killer when not used as directed. Warfarin was once used as a rat poison, and if used to poison someone who doesn't need it or administered at the wrong dose it can cause death via a fatal hemorrhage. A man was once murdered when someone intentionally gave him Warfarin for thirteen days straight. The man experienced bleeding, massive nosebleeds, and eventually died of circulatory failure.

POSSIBLY TRUE CRIME According to the *New York Times*, some studies supported the theory that former leader of the Soviet Union and Russian revolutionary Joseph Stalin died as a result of Warfarin poisoning during a dinner with members of his Politburo, but the official autopsy says stroke.

ELECTRIC GUITARS

I t's not intuitive that someone would use an electric guitar as a murder weapon (unless you count the thousands of people every year who butcher *Smoke on the Water*), but it's been known to happen. In Austin, a man beat his next-door neighbor to death with an electric guitar after a hard night of drinking, and in Forest Hill, Texas, the pastor of a local church was murdered when a man drove a car into the church, raided the music room, and began beating the pastor with an electric guitar. The police showed up and then killed the murderer with a stun gun. Not exactly the *Stairway to Heaven* anyone expected.

GOLDEN POISON DART FROG

These things pack a lot of potential murder into not much creature. Strikingly beautiful with bright yellow skin, the tiny Golden Poison Dart Frog is one of the most poisonous creatures on the planet. Its poison damages the nervous system and leads to heart failure. Indigenous to the rain forests of Colombia, these little killers average just an inch in length, yet a single little frog carries enough poison on the surface of its skin to kill ten grown adults!

DEADLY DETAILS **Native tribes surrounding the frog's natural habitat have used its batrachotoxin poison to tip the ends of their blowgun darts—hence the frog's "Poison Dart" name.**

124

TAI SHEN PEK KWAR THROAT STRIKE
(AKA "MONKEY FIST")

Tai Shen Pek Kwar is the "monkey style" kung fu seen so often in the kung fu movies of the 1970s and in animated films such as *Kung Fu Panda*. Also known as Monkey Fist, there were many different forms of monkey kung fu developed independently in ancient China. Tai Shen Pek Kwar is a difficult art to learn and practice, and there aren't many practitioners worldwide. Monkey fighters squat, flip, lunge, and dive around in a way that makes engagement tough. They strike vulnerable targets such as the knees, groin, and throat. And they can totally kill you with a throat strike using more than one method. So please don't tap on the glass.

SCIMITAR

A scimitar is a long, thin, curved sword with a single-edge blade. Some are quite thin, such as the modern adaptation of the United States Marine Corps officer's sword; others have thick, wide blades like those seen in *Lawrence of Arabia*. Persian in origin, these swords are seen as a symbol of power across the Middle East (such as in the Coat of Arms of the King of Saudi Arabia) and were known by a number of names throughout the Middle East, Southwest Asia, and what is today Turkey. They were designed so that one could slash enemies while on horseback, staying mobile without one's weapon getting stuck. These days, however, these military swords are more likely to cut through ceremonial ribbon or wedding cake.

ROCKET-PROPELLED GRENADE

An RPG is a shoulder-fired launcher that can be carried and used by just one person; it propels an explosive into a hardened military target such as an enemy tank. Muzzle-loaded and with very little recoil (pressure released into the shooter upon firing), RPGs are popular with terrorists because they're cheap, easy to use, and create a lot of hurt in not a lot of time. Good for around 300-500 meters in range, the projectile explodes after you fire it—causing nasty damage on the other end.

DEADLY DETAILS **While in the west we know the RPG as a "rocket-propelled grenade," the RPG really stands for its Russian acronym, *Ruchnoi Protivotankovye Granatamyot*.**

- - - - - - - - - MURDER MOST STRANGE - - - - - - - - -

UNOPENED CAN

Hard and heavy, that can of creamed corn or unopened soda could do more than just serve as part of dinner. It can also serve as an impromptu murder weapon! In 1999, an Alabama cashier was bludgeoned to death with a can of peas by a man who'd broken into her store to steal some money. In Staten Island, New York, a woman was arrested and charged with unlawful possession of a weapon after beating another woman in a pizzeria with an unopened soda can—though the conflict was stopped before it led to actual murder. It may sound amusing, but it's not very funny when you're on the other end of a deadly can of whoop ass!

WINCHESTER 1894

Designed by John Browning, this popular lever-action hunting rifle has put down many a game animal in the last hundred years— and many a man. Originally chambered to fire black powder cartridges, the gun evolved in many ways over its century-long legacy and grew to shoot a number of calibers through its eight-shot or six-shot tube magazine. The "Model '94" can be seen in dusty, shoot-'em-up Westerns such as *The Sons of Katie Elder*, *True Grit*, and *Rooster Cogburn*. These guns are still being manufactured to this day. Built the old fashioned way out of solid materials and using a proven design that's lasted since Thomas Edison was still alive, these guns typically last longer than their owners.

AIRPLANE "MALFUNCTION"

Sabotaging an airplane doesn't only murder a single target, but also everyone else on the plane plus anyone in the airplane's way as it crashes (and of course, all of those little bottles of vodka drunk by traveling salesmen). Numerous instances of such mass murders have occurred, such as when Flight 629 was sabotaged in 1955 via onboard explosive. The plane, a DC-6B propeller plane, went down north of

Denver, and nobody survived the crash. The saboteur? The son of a passenger on the plane. She was wealthy, well-insured and owned a successful Denver restaurant; her son planted a bomb on the plane to get his inheritance early. So the next time you find yourself complaining about your flight, remember that things could always be worse!

DEADLY DETAILS **Some conspiracy theorists think that John F. Kennedy, Jr. was killed as a result of airplane sabotage.**

- - - - - - - - - - - - - KILLER MOVES - - - - - - - - - - - - -

BAGUA CRESCENT MOON KNIFE

Crescent moon or "deer horn" knives are a traditional weapon of the kung fu Ba Gua Zhang. These rounded weapons resemble two letter Cs placed back-to-back and overlapping a little with a handle in the middle. Bagua (which translates roughly into "eight trigrams") is a type of kung fu informed by Taoist principles, and the crescent moon knives are meant to enable a practitioner to take on, defend against, and disarm multiple attackers at once. A bagua master using these murderous weapons looks like a tornado made out of razors—one you don't want to be anywhere near when it touches down.

- - - - - - - - - - PERNICIOUS POISONS - - - - - - - - - - -

POLONIUM

This rare and super-radioactive element was discovered by Marie Curie and named after her homeland of Poland. A silvery and sort-of-solid metal, it's found in uranium ores and was used in the "Fat Man" atomic bomb dropped on Nagasaki in WWII. But humans should never be around this stuff—even super small amounts can kill someone if absorbed through the skin, swallowed, or inhaled. The world's first known polonium assassination was that of Russian dissident and journalist Alexander Litvinenko, murdered by the Russian government. He'd had lunch with two Russian intelligence officers, and they put polonium in his tea—not to mention locations all around London—in what was blatantly a state-sponsored assassination. Litvinenko died three weeks later; they'd given him two hundred times more than a fatal amount (10 micrograms).

- - - - - - - - - - - **FATAL FIREARMS** - - - - - - - - - - -

LEE-ENFIELD RIFLE .303

This murderous bolt-action semi-automatic military rifle was a staple of the British military at one time, and has seen action from the Boer War to the current conflict in Afghanistan (used by insurgents this time around). When it hit the streets in 1895, the rifle shot a distinctive .303-caliber round and held a ten-round magazine loaded with clips. These guns saw a lot of service in WWII, and were eventually converted to both scoped sniper rifles and .22-caliber training rifles for cadets. Some Enfield variants had a sword bayonet mounted, especially useful in the trenches. Over seventeen million of them were made, and they worked as advertised—ending the lives of many men in many sad and faraway wars.

POP CULTURE **You can see British soldiers toting Enfields in most WWII movies, including *Saving Private Ryan*.**

KILLER ARMY ROBOTS

Military technology once meant conventional weapons such as guns and bombs. But today, exponential advances in robotics means that militaries all over the world are adapting rolling and walking robots to do all sorts of work traditionally done by soldiers—including logistics, reconnaissance, ordinance management, medical support, and, of course, breaking things and killing people. Both autonomous and remote-controlled robots of all designs are used in the field right now to gain advantage and help improve the safety of soldiers. Armed with a variety of lethal weapons systems, the defense industry is ablaze with talk of augmenting human soldiers with deadly robots of all shapes, sizes, and capabilities.

- - - - - - - - - - - - - THUG LIFE - - - - - - - - - - - - -

ACID

No good can come when you bring together human beings and certain types of acid. The grim study of homicidal behavior often reveals murderers' attempts to hide their crimes by dissolving critical evidence in acid, and sometimes acid can itself be used as a murder weapon. In one high-profile case, a Missouri woman and an accomplice murdered her estranged husband by incapacitating him with both a stun gun and chloroform—then dunking him in a bath of hydrochloric acid. The mist that forms around hydrochloric acid alone can be super-corrosive to human tissue, and the poor man never stood a chance. The woman was found guilty of first-degree murder, and sentenced to life without parole.

NUNCHUKU

Often pronounced "nun-chucks," nunchaku is a traditional martial arts weapon composed of two wooden sticks connected by a short rope or chain. These days, they come in a variety of styles, but nunchuku were originally very simple. In their native Okinawa, farmers once used these tools either to thresh rice or as horse bridles, but if attacked, the tool could then become a handy weapon. Nunchuku can be deadly on impact; the two sticks gain momentum as the fighter twirls them around his or her body, enabling powerful strikes, blocks, or the ability to grab the opponent's weapon. Whoo-pow!

fig. 1

fig. 2

fig. 3

POP CULTURE Bruce Lee made nunchuku popular in '70s kung fu flicks such as *Game of Death*, *Chinese Connection*, and *Return of the Dragon*.

131

ROLLER COASTER

I t is possible to murder someone via roller coaster, by either sabotaging the mechanics of the ride itself or by tricking someone who really shouldn't ride one to come along (such as someone with a severe heart condition). People do die on roller coasters at an alarming rate—there were approximately fifty-two roller coaster deaths reported between 1990 and 2004. But these are typically accidents; murder-by-ride is more commonly found in books and movies, like the 2006 horror flick *Final Destination 3*, which features a terrifying and deadly roller coaster.

POP CULTURE The 1970s song "Love Rollercoaster," by The Ohio Players is said to contain the scream of a woman actually being murdered—but this is just urban myth. The only carnage involving The Ohio Players was perpetrated by the dodgy accountant who butchered the band's finances and killed their careers.

- - - - - - - - - - - - - KILLER MOVES - - - - - - - - - - - - - -

TONFA

A tonfa is a traditional Okinawan martial arts weapon that dates back to the seventeenth century. At that time, the Japanese invaded Okinawa and forbade the general populace to carry weapons so that they could be more easily controlled. In response, Okinawans began carrying and using these single-handled clubs (not dissimilar in appearance to the nightsticks many police officers carry on patrol), which could be disguised as millstone handles. Today, karate practitioners use two tonfa—one in each hand—for conventional practice. It integrates into the rest of the art and enables the martial artist to take on either armed or unarmed opponents (and also to potentially whip up some killer stewed dumplings).

CARJACKING

A carjacking is where a criminal approaches a stranger's vehicle, forces the driver out (often at gunpoint), and then steals the vehicle. Not necessarily in that order. It's a grim reality that some human beings value a hunk of metal and plastic more than a human life, but there you have it. Around 38,000 carjackings happen annually in the U.S., and results vary nationwide. In many parts of the country, drivers themselves are armed and could result in carjackercide. Though experts say you should let the thieves have the car and just run, especially if you drive a Saab.

- - - - - - - - - - SLASHER MADNESS - - - - - - - - - -

BROKEN BEER BOTTLE

A lmost anytime you've got a group of people together, especially in the west, you've also got beer. Where you have beer, you often have bottles—and potential murder weapons. Victims around the world have been hit, slashed, and stabbed with bottles, largely because they tend to already be handily located where people are drinking (and possibly not making the best decisions ever). The glass from these broken bottles can be razor sharp, and many a man has lost his life to a heated exchange over one too many.

POP CULTURE   **In an episode of the cozy crime thriller Midsomer Murders called "Not in My Back Yard," a conservationist is killed with a broken bottle (presumably a "green piece" of glass).**

FURNITURE

Yep, you can murder someone with a table, chair, stool, or other seemingly harmless piece of furniture. There have been multiple incidents of people getting stabbed or beaten to death with the leg of a table in New York; in Tennessee, more than one bar patron has beaten another to death with a bar stool. And in the United Kingdom a few years ago, a man who ducked into a neighbor's house to ask him about his electric meter was almost murdered with a chair leg when the visitor insulted the resident's appearance—resulting in the rude neighbor receiving over twenty-five fractures and multiple broken bones. So if you're thinking about being rude to somebody in their own home, you may want to check the room for heavy oak first.

HAND GRENADE

A hand grenade is a small, hand-held bomb primarily used by military forces. They come in a variety of designs that do a variety of things, such as: fragmentation grenades, which fill the air with metal fragments; smoke grenades, used to signal or screen movement; concussion grenades, which kill through explosive power; and anti-tank grenades. And every one of them is capable of murder! In a British Special Operations Executive assassination known as Project Anthropoid, British operatives killed Reinhard Heydrick by blowing up his convertible with an anti-tank grenade. Heydrick played a formative role in the rise of Hitler and the Holocaust, so it couldn't have happened to a nicer guy.

IMPROVISED EXPLOSIVE DEVICE
(IED)

These terrible creations are homemade bombs deployed by trigger to catch enemy soldiers unaware, a guerilla fighting tactic used as a substitute for direct combat. The roadside bombs found in battle theaters such as Iraq and Afghanistan are examples of IEDs. These homemade bombs are highly effective in their flexibility, inexpensiveness, and ease of creation. They've been wired up to everything from abandoned cars to children's toys. Over half of the casualties incurred by coalition forces in the Afghanistan War were a result not of conventional direct combat, but rather IEDs deployed by terrorist forces.

TYPE 54

The Type 54 is a Chinese semi-automatic handgun based on an evolution of the Russian Tokarev TT-33. Norinco, the Chinese manufacturer, first made the Type 51 handgun in the 1950s. From there, the company refined the design into the 54 and other variants. Like the Tokarev, it fires a 7.62x25mm round and has either an 8-round or 14-round magazine capacity. Though now quite old, it's still in use in parts of the Chinese military and in Bangladesh. On the street in China, they're known as "Black Star" pistols and one thing is for sure: when it comes to murder, they work every bit as well as their Russian counterparts.

PUFFER FISH VENOM
(TETROTOXIN)

Tetraodontidae, commonly known as the puffer fish, is a family of smallish fish which have large spines that raise when the fish is agitated or threatened, making them appear to "puff" up. Native to the tropics, there are around 120 different varieties of puffer fish, and their meat is considered a delicacy in many parts of Asia. But certain parts of the fish—such as the liver or skin—are highly toxic and can kill by being eaten, injected, inhaled, or absorbed through the skin. The fish's venom is known as tetrotoxin, which kills via respiratory failure, and is widely believed to be the second-most poisonous venom on the face of the planet (after the Golden Poison Dart Frog, page 124).

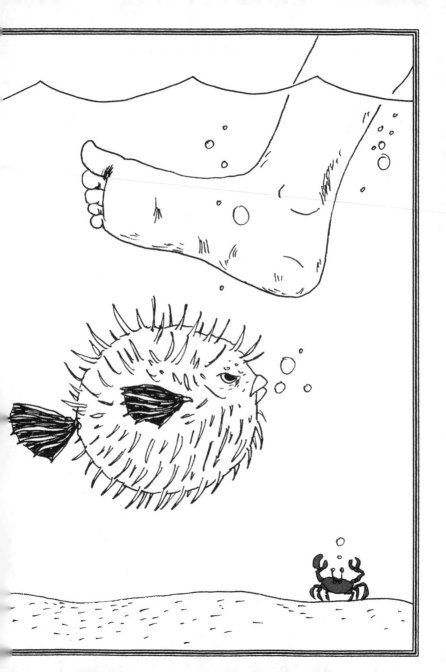

SHORT SWORD

What we know today as a short sword was first developed in the Bronze Age, around the seventeenth century BC. The metal blades have been found in the early civilizations around the Black Sea such as the Hittites and Assyrians, but when most people think of a short sword, they envision the European medieval version that consists of a small handle and hilt with a double-edged straight blade around a foot or two in length. Anything smaller would be considered a dagger, and anything longer would be a traditional long sword. Of course, getting stabbed with any of them was equally deadly. Best to keep them at the Renaissance Fair to cut Ye Old Turkey Leg.

UNDERTOW

Technically, the word "undertow" refers to a low and flat offshore-facing tidal flow that compensates for the water volume in a wave as part of it heads toward shore. What most people mean when they say "undertow" is actually rip current (also known as rip tide), which pulls people out to sea. "Accidental" drownings blamed on vicious undertow, but actually the fault of killers, are a recurring theme in books and movies. Real rip currents do kill people every year, though, because, much like arguing with a car salesman, victims simply get worn out and lose the will to fight. So you see, it doesn't always pay to "go with the flow" after all.

DEADLY DETAILS **To survive a real rip current, swim at a 90-degree angle from the shore until you're out of its grasp.**

DESERT EAGLE

The Desert Eagle is a large-caliber handgun manufactured by Magnum Research, Inc. working in conjunction with the Israeli manufacturer Israeli Military Industry. These gas-operated, semi-auto handguns can be HUGE, chambered to fire up to a .50AE-caliber round—one of the most powerful pistol rounds ever made. But you can also get them in .44, .357, and other powerfully murderous calibers. Whatever variety of models you choose, any one of them will kill someone—if you can manage to hold the gun up and aim it properly.

POP CULTURE Arnold Schwarzenegger sported one of these big mothers in his 1985 film *Commando*, and Austin Powers flashed a gold-plated Desert Eagle Mark I .357 in *Goldmember*.

- - - - - - - - - - - - KILLER MOVES - - - - - - - - - - - - -

THE WAR FAN

Concealable or dual-purpose weapons have a long legacy in martial arts. The Japanese war fan is an elegant metal fan that will cool you off just fine—possibly even permanently. Partially made of iron, Asian military officers in the field would use these fans to signal troop maneuvers in much the way European armies used signal flags. But when the fighting began, the fans could also be used to cut enemies with their razor-sharp edges. Some schools of Chinese kung fu also teach the fan as a fighting weapon, and there is a long tradition of incorporating "hidden" weapons such as the fan into ancient kung fu fighting techniques.

MOTORCYCLE CHAIN

A popular weapon with, you guessed it, outlaw biker gangs, the chain off your average, run-of-the-mill motorcycle can be a deadly weapon. There have been several thousands of motorcycles running the American roads since *Easy Rider*—so that means a lot of loose bike chains floating around junkyards and stores and garages where mechanics sport ZZ Top beards. In *Friday the 13th: Hell Lake*, psycho killer Jason Voorhees garrotes a man to death with a motorcycle chain. You can also kill someone with a bicycle chain or the chain that runs on a chainsaw. Sadly, in real life all around the United States people have been killed by all of those things.

- - - - - - - - - - - **PERNICIOUS POISONS** - - - - - - - - - - -

JIMSON WEED

D *atura stramonium*, also known as Jimson weed or datura, is a green leafy herb that grows as tall as an adult's waist. Jimson weed has white flowers and spiky asymmetrical leaves, and it contains three different types of hallucinogens: scopolamine, atropine, and hyoscyamine. Poisoning can happen by drinking tea from the leaves—which tastes terrible and could appear to have been served by your third-grade teacher wearing antlers and riding a unicorn—or by ingesting the seeds or leaf juice. Some people (bored teenagers, mostly) eat it on purpose for the mind trip, but it could all too easily end up their last trip of any kind. Potency between plants varies widely, and it's easy to overdose and die.

NINJA BLOWGUN

The ninja would sometimes murder their assigned victims by shooting them with a blowgun (known as a fukiya) whose darts had been tipped with poison. They shot the blowgun from concealed locations such as shrubs (or, presumably for the modern ninja, from behind a rack of dark suits). Ninja blowgun competitions using traditional Japanese weaponry are still held today, sans poison. But most often these days, if you find a "ninja blowgun," it's being wielded by a 10-year-old at a flea market and being shot at empty cans of Dr Pepper.

DEADLY DETAILS These deadly assassins sometimes skipped the blowgun altogether and just blew the darts from their mouths, or in the case of female ninjas, hid them in their hair. Other times, when a victim was distracted, the ninjas could simply walk up and stick the dart in by hand.

FORCED LABOR

It's entirely possible to work someone to death—and not just wait staff. This torturous means of murder has been employed by tyrannical governments, unfair cultural practices, and evil despots since the beginning of mankind. From the Soviet Gulag system that shuffled approximately 18 million prisoners through its icy gates to the Nazi exploitation of civilians for their own evil machinations (and those of corporations) to the injustice and inhumanity of slavery in the early Americas, working someone to death somehow takes more than just their life. Though we'd like to think humanity has since moved on and risen above, forced labor systems still exist in many parts of the world.

HYPOTHERMIA

W hile most cases of death by hypothermia are purely accidental, on rare occasion, murder-by-hypothermia does occur. Murderers have killed via cold by leaving bodies tied up in the trunks of cars, stuffing unfortunate victims into freezers large and small, as well as exposing unprepared people to freezing waters (even the warm waters of the Gulf of Mexico can kill someone by lowering their body temperature). Governments not-super-concerned with human rights have even employed the cold as a torture technique—keeping prison cells cold and denying prisoners clothing or blankets in what's known as "cold cell" torture. Rumors that the managers in your office building are trying to kill you with the conference room thermostat have not been substantiated.

POP CULTURE On a lighter note, if you're into murder mysteries check out *Hypothermia*—number six in Arnaldur Indridason's Reykjavik Murder Series.

SURVIVAL KNIFE

M ade popular by the movie *First Blood*, the film adaptation of the David Morrell novel, the survival knife is a large-bladed knife designed to provide tactical advantage in wilderness survival. First introduced in the nineteenth century, these specialty knives have a serrated edge on the back of the blade for use as a saw. Modern versions have a hollow handle in which you'll find matches, a whetstone, fishing line, bandages, and so forth, plus often a compass fitted into the handle itself. The military issues various higher quality versions of this knife than the popular reproduction "survival knives" sold at gun shows and shopping malls in the Midwest.

TRUE CRIME A teenager in the UK, who was being chased by three men angry at him over a debt, turned and killed one of his pursuers with a survival knife. Then he had to survive in the slammer.

- - - - - - - - - - - - **SLASHER MADNESS** - - - - - - - - - - - - - -

BUTCHER KNIFE

Millions of people have this common kitchen knife in their home, which means that millions of people have a potentially deadly weapon easily at hand. In frontier America during the 1700 and 1800s, everyone needed a large, sturdy knife to clean and dress game they caught, and while most of us no longer kill our dinners, many people still keep a butcher knife around to perform everyday kitchen duties like deboning chicken or trimming the fat off of steak. And, of course, murder. In 2015, a political extremist in the United Arab Emirates murdered an expatriate schoolteacher with a butcher knife in an upscale shopping mall. The murderer was executed by firing squad.

POP CULTURE The infamous shower scene from the classic 1960 Alfred Hitchcock film *Psycho* features a crazed Norman Bates (Anthony Perkins) stabbing young Marion Crane (Janet Leigh) to death in the shower with a butcher knife.

OLEANDER

The oleander plant is not only beautiful, but also tough—growing just as well on the side of the road as it does in a carefully monitored greenhouse. Every part of this plant contains some type of toxin, making it one of the most poisonous plants in the world! When oleander is ingested, victims first develop all kinds of terrible stomach problems, dizziness, blurred vision, and other irregularities, then are ultimately killed by acute heart problems. In 2014 a Montebello, California woman murdered her husband for insurance money by giving him a combination of oleander tea and Gatorade spiked with anti-freeze. In 1985, a woman died when mistaking oleander for eucalyptus and using it to brew tea.

144

COLT 1873

lso known as the Colt Single Action Army, this six-shot, single-action revolver has been made off and on for over 130 years. Known as "The Gun That Won the West," this flexible and reliable firearms platform was popular with lawmen, ranchers, gunfighters, soldiers, bandits, revolutionaries, and—of course—murderers. The U.S. Cavalry carried them too, and while they once represented the gritty struggle to tame the wild frontier, today they are mostly the domain of Wild West re-enactors and rare gun collectors with high-maintenance moustaches. You can easily pay tens of thousands of dollars for one of these in good condition.

- - - - - - - - - - - **SNEAKY SABOTAGE** - - - - - - - - - -

WEIGHTLIFTING "ACCIDENT"

eightlifting accidents happen. That's why it's a proven best practice to have a "spotter" with you to keep yourself safe by making sure you don't drop the weights, pull anything, or otherwise hurt yourself. But what happens if your spotter isn't exactly on your side? Such was the case a few years ago, when an Indiana man was convicted of murder after his wife was "accidentally" killed in their home gym when a weightlifting barbell with a fair amount of weight on it just happened to fall—and stay—on her throat until she departed this world due to asphyxia. With help like that, you're better off doing yoga.

KILLER DOLPHINS

Murder by dolphin? Totally flippin' possible. While U.S. citizens were watching *Flipper*, it turns out that the Soviet Union was apparently teaching marine mammals to kill divers as early as the 1960s. It's been reported that the dolphins were fitted with knives or harpoons, or were trained to drag these divers to the surface where they could be captured. While the United States government officially denies having a similar program, it's been reported that the Navy used dolphins for recon support during the war in Vietnam. And to this day, the U.S. Navy Mammal Program trains dolphins and sea lions to rescue divers, detect mines, and perform other underwater tasks.

- - - - - - - - - - - - - **KILLER MOVES** - - - - - - - - - - - - -

BATON

A baton isn't just the silver stick majorettes twirl around; it's also the name for the black, ominous-looking clubs that police officers worldwide tote around with them. Police have used these reliable, inexpensive tools to help stack the cards in their favor for years. Police departments train personnel on how to use a baton, and multiple Japanese and Filipino martial arts include a weapons curriculum that incorporates a baton-like weapon, such as the Japanese tonfa. But every once in a while they're used for out-and-out murder by all types of people.

DEADLY DETAILS The word "baton" is French for either "stick" or "day-old baguette."

UNDERWEAR

Yep. It's happened before and it will happen again—using underwear as a murder weapon. Bound to happen, really, as most of us (maybe not in Hollywood) have a pair on us all the time. Multiple serial killers have strangled female victims with the victims' own underwear, but it's happened to plenty of men too. In fact, in what is probably America's most tragic case of the "atomic wedgie," an Oklahoma man strangled his stepfather to death with his own underwear around Christmas of 2014 after everyone involved probably had a bit much to drink.

DEADLY DETAILS An "atomic wedgie" (scourge of the fraternity house though typically not fatal) is where one pulls the elastic band from a guy's underwear up over the victim's head and around his neck.

- - - - - - - - - - **PERNICIOUS POISONS** - - - - - - - - - -

LEAD

Poisoning someone with lead is murder in more ways than one; you damage the victim's health, but you can also make them crazy and mean. Exposing someone to lead via food, drink, soil, or even air can result in muscle pain, difficulty thinking, headaches, damage to the nervous system, and other serious symptoms (including, well, death). In addition, scientists have proven a link between violent crimes such as murder and the amount of lead-based paint and gasoline used in a community. Over the course of 20 years, counties in the United States with the highest instances of lead pollution experienced a four-fold increase in homicides. And it's worth mentioning, of course, that most bullets are made of lead—a different kind of lead poisoning.

HAMMER

The hammer was invented somewhere around 2.6 million BC. And for almost as long, they've been used to build crime scenes in addition to items of benefit to humanity. Their omnipresence, affordability, and deadly potential mean that countless murders worldwide have been committed via blunt force trauma using a hammer. The most prolific and dastardly was probably Indian serial killer Kampatimar Shankariya, who was convicted of killing more than seventy people with a hammer (not all at once), and was charged in 1979. During 2011, there were 496 murders committed with either hammers or makeshift clubs, and only 323 murders with rifles. So we beg of you, in the name of all that is holy: Please don't hurt 'em, hammer.

- - - - - - - - - - - - SLASHER MADNESS - - - - - - - - - - - -

KEYS

Sharp and easily available, keys make perfectly plausible murder weapons. People seem to get stabbed a lot with keys, often in heat-of-the-moment arguments—though few succumb to their injuries in a fatal manner, you could catch tetanus or another disease by getting cut from a dirty key. It's also possible to bludgeon someone with a very large set of keys on a chain, such as those carried by maintenance personnel on the job. And a lock on a chain can also be a deadly weapon in the right (or wrong) hands, swinging it around like a flail. So careful what you do with those keys, or you might wind up under lock and key yourself.

NINJA THROWING STARS

Technically known as a *shuriken*, the "throwing star" is a flat bladed or spiked object thrown at an opponent. The stars come in a variety of shapes and sizes, some resembling discs, coins, and spikes or a series of spikes. A weapon of the ancient *ninjutsu* martial art, shuriken were used in conjunction with swords to distract the enemy during battle, though it is still technically possible to murder someone with them, especially if the shuriken were coated with poison or unsanitary bacteria. Check out the 1981 film *Enter the Ninja* with Sho Kosugi to see flying ninja death stars aplenty!

149

BLACK POWDER RIFLES

O ne of the earliest guns in existence, a black powder rifle is a long gun where one pours the gunpowder down the muzzle and performs a bunch of other time-consuming jiggery-pokery before it could eventually fire a single lead ball. Just one at a time—in order to fire a second shot, one had to do the whole ritual all over again: clean it, pour the powder, load it, tamp it down, etc. Many of the restrictive federal laws applying to modern firearms don't apply to black powder weapons, so just about anyone can buy one (though not everyone can figure out how to actually use one).

DEADLY DETAILS You can still buy these guns, popular with historical re-enactors, at sporting goods stores.

DIMETHYLMERCURY

D imethylmercury is the most toxic form of mercury on the planet. One of the most potent neurotoxins known to man, this organo-metallic compound isn't good for much but murder. As little as one cubic centimeter (about the size of a grape) will kill you deader than a sack of tacks. Even lab gloves won't protect you from it; dimethylmercury can pass right through them. Case in point, a renowned professor of chemistry at Dartmouth College was accidentally exposed to a just a tiny amount of dimethylmercury when it was absorbed through her lab gloves. A few months later, she fell ill—and ten months after that, she passed on.

STUCK DOWN A WELL

Somebody throws you down a well in the middle of nowhere. You can't get out. Whatcha gonna do? Well, you'll probably end up a murder victim. Leaving someone in a well to die dates back to Biblical times. And it still happens, mostly in developing countries (where there are more wells in the middle of more nowhere). Wells can also be used as handy places to dispose of a murder victim after murdering them in some other way. So be careful where you get your water—or where you make a wish.

- - - - - - - - - - - - THUG LIFE - - - - - - - - - - - -

ICE PICK

Ice picks look like screwdrivers, only with a pointed end, and were more common back in the day when ice was sold from "ice houses" and delivered to your house in blocks. You had to use the picks to chip off pieces of ice (before everyone's refrigerator dispensed chipped ice on demand). A number of mafia hit men—and just plain crazy people—have used ice picks as effective murder weapons; and if you see an ice pick in a movie, chances are somebody will be murdered with it later on in the film. In the 1992 film *Basic Instinct* with Michael Douglas and Sharon Stone, the killer stabbed victims with an ice pick during sex (talk about cold).

TRUE CRIME **Russian revolutionary Leon Trotsky was murdered with an ice axe—a long, thin axe resembling an ice pick— while in exile in Mexico. Yeah, nothing suspicious about an ice axe in Mexico.**

ELECTROCUTION BY LAMP

We take for granted all of the live-wire electricity running around our homes. At 120 volts (or 220 depending on your country of residence), all of this power may be convenient—but it can also be deadly. Murder by lamp means rewiring a lamp so that anyone touching it will experience an electric shock severe enough to make the heart spasm, and can result in death. Taking a certain level of electrical current to the body actually produces a cardiac arrest, a frighteningly simple murder method for someone who knows basic electrical principles. In 2010, an investigation revealed that a mysterious hit squad murdered a Hamas commander in a Dubai hotel by sabotaging his bedside lamp.

JAPANESE TANTO

The tanto is a traditional Japanese short knife, worn by the samurai to complement the warrior's long and short swords. The tanto's blade has a distinctive design and construction, which was said to have been capable of penetrating weak spots in the armor of its day. These high-quality, intricately made knives date back to around 1,000AD and were typically a foot long or less with a sharp point and a single sharp edge. They will murder someone faster than you could say Banzai! Artfully crafted in a variety of styles, what most people know as a tanto knife today often had a about 45-degree blade angle at the end of the knife. In addition to samurai, women also carried them for self-defense. Today, any knife with a blade similarly styled is known as a tanto knife—and many hold out that the tanto blade shape still brings extra piercing power.

- - - - - - - - - - - - - - - **THUG LIFE** - - - - - - - - - - - - -

SHOVEL

Shovels have been used to both send people to their graves and dig the actual hole. It doesn't take many pounds of pressure per square inch to kill someone with a big swing. Yet still, both in fiction and real life, people get hit in the head using shovels with astonishing frequency. (In the land of fiction and film production, some people call this trope "the travelling shovel of death" because it appears in plots so frequently.) From *Midsomer Murders* to the real-life, cold-blooded 2010 Atlanta killing of a young landscaper by his wife and her lover—if you have a shovel, best keep careful track of it.

SYSTEMA KNIFE TECHNIQUES

Systema (literally "the system" in Russian) is a Russian martial arts style that was adopted by the Soviet Special Forces (*Spetnaz*), as well as the KGB. This pragmatic style combines striking with grappling, joint lock manipulation, and weapons training all geared around ending a hand-to-hand engagement quickly. Among its many competencies are some murderously deadly knife-fighting techniques. Systema fighters learn to disarm knife-wielding attackers, slice people up six ways to Sunday, grapple with armed or multiple attackers, and just generally defeat someone with their overall badassery. Systema isn't just deadly—it also looks cool, and more and more Russian hand-to-hand combat has been recently used in Hollywood fight choreography.

- - - - - - - - - - - - **FATAL FIREARMS** - - - - - - - - - - - -

"MA DEUCE" BMG .50

To make killing easier is the whole point of the M2 Browning 50-caliber machine gun. In the field since the early 1930s, this thunderous beast makes a massive hole in anything in its way. Several holes, actually, as it can fire hundreds of rounds per minute. It's used to support infantry, take down aircraft, shoot from an aircraft—or just generally scare the crap out of anyone. It's even used as a sniper rifle; legendary sharpshooter Carlos Hathcock made a confirmed kill with an M2 at 2,460 yards during the Vietnam War (that's the length of a couple dozen football fields). Its design has been refined, but is much unchanged, and the weapon is still used by the military today.

STEAK KNIFE

Not just the purview of *Murder, She Wrote*, unfortunate real world victims are stabbed to death with steak knives all the time. Indeed, these infamous implements always seem to be in the wrong place at the wrong time. In New York, a 49-year-old man was once stabbed to death with a steak knife over an argument at a barbeque. So keep your dinner chat civil!

DEADLY DETAILS "Stakeknife" sic was also the codename of a British spy during The Troubles with Northern Ireland, who infiltrated the IRA and gathered critical intelligence in the fight against terrorism.

- - - - - - - - - - - - - **KILLER MOVES** - - - - - - - - - - - - -

AIKIDO HEAD SLAM

The Japanese martial art of Aikido is built on a pacifist philosophy: the more energy an opponent uses against you, the more you'll redirect back at them by means of throws, joint locks, and strikes. So your opponent is only safe if they don't attack you. But when engaged, a number of Aikido techniques can be totally murderous (and not just in Aikido expert Steven Segal's 1990 film *Marked for Death*). Even one of the system's most basic throws, *shomenuchi iriminage*, which looks sort of like a wrestling clothesline if you miss the finer points, can plant someone's head on the concrete and end their life.

KILLER BEES

I f you're allergic to bee stings, it won't take more than one or two to kill you; but anyone can die from bee stings if they're stung enough times (3,000 in the case of one Texas man). Bees communicate through smell, and apparently the message "attack this person" smells a lot like bananas. Yup. If someone smells like bananas—if he or she just ate one, or used banana-scented shampoo that morning, whatever—the hive will attack! So if your husband stuffs bananas in your purse and pushes you near a beehive, better check your life insurance coverage.

POP CULTURE In the 1993 film *The Crush*, a young Alicia Silverstone tries to kill a perceived rival by piping bees into a photographer's darkroom.

VITAMINS

B elieve it or not, making someone OD on vitamins could make you a murderer. Hypervitaminosis is the term for too much of a good thing on the vitamin front. For instance, Hypervitaminosis D can be contracted from milk that's been overly fortified or contains too many supplements—and can be deadly. It is a tough way to kill, however, since hypervitaminosis is a cumulative condition and the victim would likely recognize symptoms far before his or her situation were critical. However, if you were to convince your victim to eat the liver of a polar bear, that could give him or her an acute case of Hypervitaminosis A, and could cause coma or death.

THROWING KNIFE

A throwing knife is a medium-sized double-edged knife that's well-balanced for throwing, as the name implies. Developed independently in many different places around the world, a throwing knife gives combatants the option to fight at close range or to chance a thrown blade to achieve a distance advantage. While it's actually quite tricky to murder someone with a throwing knife because of the technical difficulty and their relative light weight, it's not unheard of for a knife-throwing act to turn deadly—although not as often as it's seen in the movies, where circus performers, assassins, ninjas, and other dexterous killers pin their victims with throwing knives like they were starting a deadly bug collection.

- - - - - - - - - - - - FATAL FIREARMS - - - - - - - - - - - -

AR-15

What most people know as an "AR-15" is just the civilian version of the military's standard issue M-16 service rifle. These come standard chambered in .233/5.56 caliber and are semi-automatic (one trigger pull means one shot, not a continuous spray of hellfire). Most people use them to plink at the range, for home defense or to hunt. But, occasionally, they're also used for murder. Colt actually bought the name "AR" from ArmaLite (from which the AR acronym is derived). But like Coke and Xerox, the name has been commoditized to mean any civilian, semi-automatic small caliber long gun that looks like the old M16 rifle. They look like the rifles carried by American forces in *Apocalypse Now* and other Vietnam-era flicks.

R*A*T POISON

They say that in any major city you're never more than six feet away from a rat. Which makes rat poison not only handy for pest control, but also for murder. Rat poison has been made from a number of different chemicals over the years, including arsenic, thallium, and strychnine; none of which are good for you. Modern rat poison is often made of brodifacoum, which doesn't kill immediately but takes a bit of time; this is so the rodent won't die immediately and its little friends don't associate the death with the poison.

You know, so they don't smell a rat.

TRUE CRIME In 1954, Nannie Doss (also known as "Arsenic Annie" and "Giggling Granny") was convicted of putting rat poison over prunes and then feeding them to people in her family she didn't like—she confessed to killing four of her five husbands, and was suspected of also having poisoned a mother-in-law, her own mother and sister, and several of her children, among others.

PITCHFORK

Oh, *American Gothic*, how far you have fallen. The pitchfork is basically a long-handled fork-like tool with three or four thick, long prongs on the end. Typically made of wood with a steel handle, they were used to throw (pitch) hay on farms. But, of course, those long and sharp prongs can result in big *tine* murder. Although he spared the patrons' lives, a Tennessee man was arrested in 2014 for allegedly using a pitchfork to rob a Waffle House. And throw in those pigs-in-a-blanket with some maple syrup while you're at it! Move, damn it! Move!

POP CULTURE

In the *Midsomer Murders* episode "Judgment Day," the team investigates when a local ne'er-do-well is murdered with a pitchfork; nobody gets away from those guys.

SMALLPOX

Murder via smallpox is a historical fact. What we call smallpox is an infectious disease cause by the Variola virus ("pox" is Latin for spotted, referring to the blisters that occur on those infected with the disease). Victims get symptoms of the flu, the telltale rash, and—in about 30 percent of cases—death. There is no cure. A number of people have been intentionally murdered through the exposure to the disease; the Soviet Union killed several people via smallpox in 1971 by way of experiment. Britain was the first nation to conceive of weaponizing the disease through contaminated blankets given to Native Americans who were at the time allied with France. Naturally occurring smallpox was actually all but eradicated by the 1980s, and today it exists mostly in laboratories. Thank goodness.

BETA BLOCKERS

This class of pharmaceutical is used to treat everything from heart conditions to migraine headaches by interfering with receptors that allow the heart and other organs to process the hormones that come from stress. But giving someone too much will cause heart irregularities, low blood pressure, and death. In the famous trial of Claus Von Bulow, beta-blockers were found to have contributed to his wife Sunny Von Bulow's descent into a coma from which she never awoke. Her husband was suspected of poisoning her, but was eventually acquitted—and turned into a brilliant performance by Jeremy Irons in the 1990 movie about the trial, *Reversal of Fortune*.

HENRY REPEATING RIFLE

This legendary rifle came out right around the same time that the Civil War began. The gun is a lever-action that feeds from a 16-round tube magazine (plus one in the chamber)—which was quite a high capacity at the time. A skilled operator could get off twenty-eight rounds per minute with the gun, and these rifles went a long way toward tipping many engagements in favor of Northern forces. They were also used in subsequent frontier fighting against tribes of Native Americans. And, of course, murder. These days, though available in a more accessible caliber, the guns are mostly used by Cowboy Shooters (competitive Wild West style hobbyists) and war re-enactors.

- - - - - - - - - - - - SLASHER MADNESS - - - - - - - - - - -

MULTI-TOOL

A multi-tool is a compact, flat utility knife with two square handles which conceal a variety of tools such as knife blades, screw drivers, bottle openers, pliers, and more. Unfortunately, they're also used not just to fix things but also to make them worse—via murder. After the launch of the popular multi-tool brand, the Leatherman, these handy devices made their way around the world. Alas, not everyone tooled responsibly. A number of people have been stabbed to death with multi-tools, including a woman in Reno in 2013 and a mother—by her own daughter—in California in 2010. And in February of 2014, a jealous boyfriend in the United Kingdom murdered his girlfriend with a Swiss army knife after discovering she was screwing around. (See what we did there?)

CURLING IRON

Both hot and electrical, curling irons—those handy tools of the beauty trade—can bring new meaning to the phrase "curl up and die." These things are just all-around dangerous; not only do they look like little clubs but also they can heat up to 400 degrees! In 2012, a college student arguing with his girlfriend beat her to death with a curling iron. And in the (campy indeed) 1983 horror flick *Sleepaway Camp*, one unfortunate victim was murdered when the killer placed a curling iron where…typically curling irons don't go (think *Canterbury Tales*).

NAPALM

This murderous concoction is part gel and part fuel, and when deployed as an incendiary device, it will not only burn people and things but also stick to them to make sure they stay burned. As an anti-personnel weapon, napalm adheres to its victims and exposes them to temperatures up to over 2,000 degrees Fahrenheit (water boils at 212F). Developed at Harvard during WWII, its ingredients include polystyrene (as the thickening agent), hydrocarbon benzene (super-potent jet fuel) and gasoline. It was used extensively in the Pacific theatre, later in the conflict in Korea and then for several years in Vietnam. Napalm is also an alleged carcinogen, and many people exposed to it may have developed cancer as a side effect.

EAGLE CLAW

Eagle Claw (also known as Ying Zhoa Tang Lang) is a traditional kung fu style that dates back to the Chinese general Yue Fie in the 1100s, and was handed down from a succession of Shaolin monks. This traditional Northern Chinese kung fu style is composed of potentially deadly strikes and kicks, joint locks, and trapping/throwing techniques. A number of these techniques are capable of killing someone, especially its "throat claw" that cuts off the flow of air and typically damages the larynx as collateral damage. Caw!

POP CULTURE You can see Eagle Claw kung fu and its deadly talons in action during the 1978 Taiwanese feature film *Eagle's Claw*, where fists are flying and fighters are dying left and right.

- - - - - - - - - - - PERNICIOUS POISONS - - - - - - - - - - -

THE "V" OF DEATH

In 2013, a Brazilian woman attempted to murder her husband by pouring poison in her girly parts and then persuading her husband to give her oral sex. Apparently she was angry because he wouldn't grant her a divorce. But the murder didn't go down as planned: the husband was concerned about the strange odor emanating from his wife, and in a fit of concern drove her to the hospital. Both survived, but presumably the marriage was DOA. Though her cunning murder plot might have worked if the man was less observant, the poison likely would have also killed the wife, since the human body's more sensitive bits tend to be quite absorbent.

SAW

A saw is a manual tool used to cut things via a serrated blade, chain, wire, or other cutting surface. Though the Greeks and Chinese both credit themselves with inventing it, the earliest saws on record are Egyptian copper affairs dating back to around 3,000BC. Though many people are hurt or killed by saws accidentally, surprisingly few were used to kill until the horror film franchise *Saw* popularized the saw as a murder weapon for modern audiences, and spurned unfortunate copycat killings such as the brutal murder of a soldier by a crazed man in the United Kingdom who'd seen the movies. (Most people who see the *Saw* movies are only hurting themselves.)

- - - - - - - - - - - - FATAL FIREARMS - - - - - - - - - - - -

HI-POINT HANDGUNS

People responsibly use guns made by Hi-Point Firearms every day for hunting, home defense, or just plinking at the range. Of course, they could also potentially be used to kill. And one of the things that makes them an attractive murder weapon is price. They're some of the most inexpensive guns on the planet. You can buy five or six Hi-Point handguns for the price of one upmarket gun of the same caliber. So for murderers looking for a throwaway gun (or crooked cops in a movie looking for a "throw down piece"), the Hi-Point handgun is where it's at. And don't think that these guns are junk just because they're cheap—the company offers a lifetime warranty!

DEADLY SNAKES

Though Indiana Jones managed to escape this unpleasant demise, it is totally possible to murder someone by putting them in proximity to venomous snakes. Probably much rarer in real life than on television and the movies, placing a venomous snake in somebody's bed, car, or other personal space could have deadly results indeed. The snake with the most murderous potential is likely the Inland Taipan, a native of Australia whose venom is specifically designed to kill mammals (like us, for example). Its bite is said to have enough killing power to put a hundred men in their graves!

POP CULTURE In one of Sir Arthur Conan Doyle's Sherlock Holmes tales, *The Speckled Band*, the villain trains a deadly snake to seek out victims to further his murderous aims.

TRAIN "ACCIDENT"

With all the high-speed trains hurtling down all the metal tracks around the world, someone is bound to get killed. Of course, sometimes these aren't accidents—sometimes it's sabotage. One relatively common tactic used by everyone from Butch Cassidy to modern-day bad guys is to derail a train by damaging the tracks in advance prior to the train's arrival. The Wilcox Train robbery, whereby bandits blew a bridge between two sections of a train is one of the most famous. The bandits allegedly got away with more than $50,000 in loot, including "19 scarf pins." Huh?

TRUE CRIME **While nobody died in the process, hundreds of lives were risked by a UK train worker's thirst for cash. The InterCity train had a policy that if a train was delayed for more than an hour, passengers were entitled to a free drink. So one of the railcar workers kept sabotaging the trains and serving drinks—charging customers full price and pocketing the money! He put nine different trains out of service over the course of his scam.**

BUTTER KNIFE

Ican't believe it's not murder! These knives are in every cutlery drawer; disposable plastic versions even come free with your take-away. They're not sharp at all. And yet, people still manage to use them as murder weapons. In 2006, a nursing assistant, whose husband had beaten her repeatedly, had enough one day and plunged a butter knife into his heart (she was later acquitted of his murder). And in 2013 a Canadian man too drunk to defend himself was also killed after being stabbed in the heart with a butter knife. The prospect of being murdered with a dull knife seems more torturous than being killed with a sharp one that would do the job quickly.

- - - - - - - - - - **PERNICIOUS POISONS** - - - - - - - - - - -

TOXIC WASTE

It's entirely possible to murder someone by exposing them to toxic industrial waste. When potentially harmful waste materials are disposed of improperly, they can contaminate the environment, food sources, and water supplies—causing death and a host of illnesses. In 2011, a petition was filed in a Dutch court to bring murder charges against employees of an industrial company accused of mishandling toxic sludge in Abidjan, Cote d'Ivoire. And in Southern Italy, a new brand of "ecomafia" is terrorizing an area north of Naples called "the triangle of death," after a spate of cancer-related deaths and other illnesses began occurring near illegally dumped toxic waste sites.

TRUE CRIME In Germany in 2001, an employee of a nuclear waste reprocessing plant stole rags used to wipe up liquid plutonium waste from around the plant. His plan was to give his ex-wife radiation poisoning, though he was caught and she survived. The state spent about two million Euros cleaning up all of the contamination from the rags (though, presumably, nothing could clean up their marriage).

KA-BAR

The KA-BAR knife was the official combat and utility knife issued to the United States Marine Corps deployed during WWII. A big, mean-looking sucker with about a seven-inch, straight, single-edged blade and a wrapped leather handle, it's gone through many iterations over the years. Eventually the U.S. Army and U.S. Navy both also adopted the knife, which in addition to being a deadly weapon can also be used to dig holes, open cans, cut wire, and open packages of beef jerky.

DEADLY DETAILS **Rumor has it that the name came from a letter written by a fur trapper who'd used one to kill a bear when his rifle jammed. But the letter was only partially legible, and "ka bar" was all they could make out.**

COFFEE MUG

Some people can't get up in the morning without their favorite coffee cup. But for others, a hot cup of coffee is the last thing they'll ever see! Their significant weight as an impact weapon (and potentially sharp edges when broken) make using coffee mugs a perfectly viable means of murder. In 2013, a Japanese housewife beat her husband to death with a coffee mug—hitting him ten times in the head—after learning that he'd slept with another woman. "He had an affair with a woman I hate," she told police by way of explanation. And they say revenge is best served up cold!

SPEAR

One of the man's earliest weapons (the oldest known date back 400,000 years), your basic spear typically involves a pole shaft with a pointed metal head. This simple weapon can be used to kill quickly and efficiently, and was incorporated into traditional Chinese martial arts around the time of the Ming Dynasty (1368-1644). Martial artists from Chinese, Korean, Japanese, and Filipino fighting styles have all at one time used spears in combat, and even the fighting monks of the Shaolin Temple often trained to fight with a spear.

PACEMAKER "PROBLEM"

People with pacemakers are (not so surprisingly) also susceptible to additional health risks—including the risk of murder. Because there's so much technology in a modern pacemaker, it's possible to intentionally cause one to malfunction, killing an individual, or for a savvy computer hacker to kill multiple pacemaker users at once by introducing malware into proprietary healthcare computer systems. On the other hand, murder cases have been encountered whereby a murder victim's time of death has been accurately recorded via pacemaker—helping investigators solve the crime.

POP CULTURE John Rain, the uber-deadly assassin in Barry Eisler's thriller novels, once sabotaged a subject's pacemaker via remote-control to fulfill a contract to kill.

171

DUCK'S FOOT PISTOL

A product of the 18th century, the duck's foot pistol was a flintlock pistol with a single grip, a single trigger—but four different barrels splaying out side-by-side from the handle like a fan. It derives its name from its shape, and fired a bullet from each of the four barrels. The concept behind the gun was to provide tactical advantage to an individual who was firing into a crowd. While all but impossible to aim the gun directly at a target, it was commonly carried by high-ranking members of a ship's crew in case of a mutiny. The duck's foot barrel was actually an attachment that transformed certain conventional flintlocks into tools of multiple murder.

- - - - - - - - - - - - - KILLER MOVES - - - - - - - - - - - - -

KRAV MAGA

K rav Maga is a deadly martial art developed by the Israeli Defense Forces. A modern, hybrid fighting style, it integrates the strengths of several traditional martial arts as well as new techniques that address contemporary defense situations. And their reality-based training protocols mean that Krav Maga fighters aren't just formidable—they're downright dangerous. From punching an attacker in the throat to disarming someone with a loaded gun (or even a hand grenade!), this brutal fighting system has the potential to murder all day long if in the wrong hands.

POP CULTURE You can see people using Krav Maga in movies such as *Taken*, *Blood Diamond*, and *Casino Royale*.

CROWBAR

A crowbar is a heavy metal iron bar that's flat on both ends and used to pry things open. Swing-able with one hand and easy to carry around, they're also formidable makeshift weapons once popular with biker gangs, though few people actually have crowbars in their homes these days. In one tragic crowbar murder, an ill man who legally grew medical marijuana in his shed was beaten with a crowbar when thieves tried to rob him of his crop. When the police arrived, they spent a lot of time asking the barely conscious victim questions about his pot shed and not much time attending to his crowbar-inflicted injuries. He died as a result.

APACHE REVOLVER

A round 1900, a shady group who called themselves "Les Apaches" frequented the criminal underground of Paris, France. This group was known for carrying slim, scary-looking revolvers which also incorporated both a knife and a set of brass knuckles (which served as the handle of the gun). Made in the 1800s and designed by a Frenchman named Louis Doine, these deadly (and frankly ridiculously impractical) guns looked like they'd been designed by a 13-year-old. Only good at point-blank range, they have no barrel and fire right from the chamber. The Apache Revolver had no safety mechanisms at all, and was probably as dangerous to its owner as it was to an intended victim. Les Apaches fizzled out around WWI, but the Apache revolver was adapted by British commandos for a brief time in the war.

HYDROGEN CYANIDE

This inorganic liquid is a valuable feedstock (the raw chemicals used to make useful products) in manufacturing commodities including plastic, pharmaceuticals, and nylon. It's used in numerous industrial processes too. But it's also super-toxic and can kill someone deader than disco. When consumed, cyanide inhibits a critical enzyme that helps the body produce energy—eventually cratering the heart and nervous system. So deadly is hydrogen cyanide that this is the "suicide pill" you see given to spies in the movies in case they are caught. The leadership of the German Third Reich—including Adolph Hitler, Eva Braun, Heinrich Himmler, and Hermann Goring—all committed suicide via hydrogen cyanide pills (Hitler took hydrogen cyanide and then shot himself, just to be sure). Cheerful thought: Manufacturing facilities around the world make enough hydrogen cyanide monthly to kill every person on the planet.

SUICIDE BOMBERS

Few things are as lethal as a human being with nothing to lose. Suicide bombers turn themselves into deadly weapons by strapping hidden explosives to their bodies and gaining access to a predetermined target, either for the purposes of killing a specific individual, or just causing fear and panic in general. The use of human beings as explosive guidance systems dates back to Imperialist Russia. Today, fanatics of all shapes and sizes employ this tactic—typically either as a means of indiscriminate assassination or to disrupt civilian life in the name of a political cause. Terrorist groups often employ the tactic to maximize public fear. In 2014 alone, there were 592 suicide bomb attacks.

TRUE CRIME In 1999, three Palestinian terrorists prematurely blew themselves up driving down the road because their timers were set for Daylight Savings Time.

- - - - - - - - - - - - SLASHER MADNESS - - - - - - - - - - - -

ARTS AND CRAFTS KNIFE

These round-body aluminum knives have a small, sharp, angled blade on the end of a metal pen-like holder that's been used for meticulous cutting since its original invention as a surgical tool in 1917, and is beloved by artists, hobbyists, architects—and, of course, killers. Because they're so sharp, can be handled with such precision, and can be found in any craft shop, it's absolutely possible to use a wee knife like this as a murder weapon. Charles Albright, a Texan serial killer known as "The Eyeball Killer," used an arts and crafts knife to perform his grim, obscene work. And also in Texas, a community college student went on a stabbing spree and stabbed fourteen people around campus before being apprehended.

- - - - - - - - - - - - SNEAKY SABOTAGE - - - - - - - - - - - -

STARVATION

Killing someone by denying them food is one of the oldest and most cruel murder methods known to mankind. The young, disabled, and elderly are especially susceptible to such crimes, as they are often dependent on caregivers. In the 1930s, Soviet leaders appropriated private farms and brought them under collective control (which means mismanagement), and intentionally allowed millions of people to starve. Hitler also used starvation as a weapon against his political enemies and prisoners.

TRUE CRIME In ancient Rome, the Imperial princess Agrippina the Elder—mother of Caligula and grandmother of Nero—was starved to death while exiled on the island of Pandateria (today, the island is known as Ventotene and she could have just found a Starbucks or something).

- - - - - - - - - - - FATAL FIREARMS - - - - - - - - - - - -

MAGPUL FMG9

This snazzy little carbine is a folding submachine gun chambered in 9/19mm parabellum (a common handgun round found everywhere) and sporting a magazine capacity of over 30 rounds. Magpul Industries is better known for its high-performance firearm accessories (such as its Magpul magazines, the gold standard for high-performance, high-capacity magazines for AR-style and other popular guns), but in the case of the FMG9, Magpul was the original equipment manufacturer of this murderous little weapon. The gun, which folds up to a fraction of its size, was meant to be a high-capacity conceal gun and made of polymer rather than metal. The FMG9 is super popular in the gaming world, making appearances in *Call of Duty: Modern Warfare 3*, *Rainbow 6: Siege*, and *Battlefield Hardline*.

DEADLY DETAILS This foldable firearm was so compact in its concealed mode that it would fit into the back pocket of a man's jeans

CLIFF or MOUNTAIN FALL

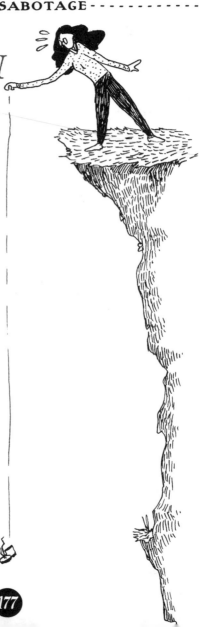

People really do get killed when they're unsafe or unlucky hiking around cliffs and canyons. But sometimes those people have a little help. In 2014, a pair of newlyweds decided to take in the sights at the beautiful Glacier National Park in Montana—only the young bride of eight days seemed to have her sights set on murder instead, and pushed her husband off a cliff, hundreds of feet above a rocky ravine. And in 2015, a man was found guilty of pushing his wife off of a cliff in Colorado's Rocky Mountain National Park to snag $4.7 million in payouts from insurance. How's that for a lover's leap?

MISCHIEF AT SEA

From sailboats to ocean liners, tampering with somebody's boat could absolutely result in murder. And it's more common than you'd think, especially during times of war. For instance, during the Civil War, a steamboat called the Sultana exploded on the Mississippi—many say the work of a Confederate sympathizer. The boat was filled with Northern soldiers heading home after the war, and the man purportedly planted a "coal torpedo," a hollow piece of iron with an explosive inside, into the ship's boiler. The explosion killed approximately 1,800 soldiers. Sabotage has been widely used for political purposes, against everyone from wealthy yachtsmen to asylum seekers.

TRUE CRIME In 2015, a young New York woman was charged with the murder of her fiancé by sabotaging his kayak.

ELECTRIC KNIFE

An electric knife is a handy contraption with two serrated blades that saw back and forth in tandem, making both carving the Thanksgiving turkey and killing that special someone all the easier. One of the most notorious such murders took place in Iraq. Uday Hussein, Saddam Hussein's eldest son, had a reputation as a sadistic psychopath, which was solidified in 1988 when—in full view of a crowd of dignitaries during a formal event with the then Egyptian President's wife—a drunken Uday attacked one of his father's bodyguards and murdered the poor man with an electric knife. (The very rude party guest's electric knife wasn't much help in 2003, however, when the United States Army 101st Airborne Division came calling.)

TIRE TOOL

A tire tool is a small but heavy angled iron rod used to remove tires and wheels from vehicles. Your average tire tool these days weighs about five pounds. Murderers typically use them to bludgeon their victims to death, since they're hefty and handy (a lot of people drive around with one in their trunk; some tire tools even come with the car when you buy it). In 2011, a Kentucky woman used a tire tool to beat her boyfriend to death after a heated argument (plus lots and lots of liquor).

NINJA SHUKO CLAWS

Strapped onto the hand like gloves, the shuko are metal claws extending from the palms designed to help ninja climb more easily. But they could just as easily help them commit murder. To kill someone with the shuko, one would use the claws to tear at the opponent's throat—specifically the jugular. They could also be topped with a poison that could kill or sicken your enemy after a hand-to-hand engagement. The downside of wearing the ninja shuko is that it's difficult to handle weapons while they're on, so a ninja would have to remove them to engage in truly effective combat. Also, you probably shouldn't go scratching your nether regions while wearing these bad boys.

ATTACK MONKEYS

Monkeys are both smart and strong—and fully capable of murder. In 2009, a monkey who was mistreated by its owner snapped and killed the man by throwing a coconut at him from atop a tree, and *The Guardian* reported in 2000 that Parisian street gangs were training monkeys smuggled in from Africa to attack unsuspecting victims. Even militaries recognizes simian killing skills; the Chinese People's Liberation Army has trained attack monkeys to scuttle up trees and kill birds that could potentially bring down planes by getting sucked into their engines. And Marvel Comics actually created a character called Hit Monkey, a little furry assassin. Awww.

DRAGON WING ELBOW STRIKE

A "dragon wing" elbow strike is performed when the martial artist puts his or her entire bodyweight into an elbow strike—rotating the hips and throwing the elbow horizontally. When striking full force to the head or neck, it's every bit possible that the strike could result in death. Getting hit with a well-thrown elbow is like getting hit with a baseball bat. Even big, tough UFC guys can get taken out with an elbow strike. It's also a dangerous technique because the recipient could be knocked out and hit their head as they land on the concrete or floor. In 2014, a mixed martial arts cage fighter was killed in the ring with an elbow strike. Research into the potential lethality of the Chicken Wing technique is still ongoing.

- - - - - - - - - - - PERNICIOUS POISONS - - - - - - - - - - -

CHLORINE GAS

Most people associate chlorine with their swimming pool, but this element can kill more than just a few hours on a summer afternoon. Under normal conditions, chlorine is sort of a yellow-green gas. It's rarely found naturally on earth in its pure form, though chlorine compounds (such as table salt) are everywhere. First used as a chemical weapon by the Germans during WWI, chlorine gas attacks the respiratory system when inhaled; it reacts with your body to turn itself into acid. Even deadlier, chlorine gas can be explosive when mixed with ammonia!

NEOSTEAD 2000

L ooking like something that came from the future, the Neostead 2000 is a combat 12-guage shotgun—capable of holding 12 rounds via two 6-shot tube magazines. The operator can choose between less-than-lethal rounds and conventional loads if needed. It's short, with magazines behind the trigger bull-pup style. The Neostead is easy to handle in urban, close-quarters engagements. It's also relatively rare, seen in only limited use in Europe and its native South Africa. The United States prohibits the sale of them at home because the Bureau of Alcohol, Tobacco and Firearms prefers citizens only have "sporting guns," and this one makes them a little nervous.

CLUB

W hen you see children's cartoons where a caveman is holding a wooden club, that's pretty factually accurate. Man has used a club to kill since prehistoric times— the *Homo habilis* species, which lived over a million years ago during the Gelasian Pleistocene period, used clubs as weapons—and over the millennia, they've since been constructed using a variety of different design variations and materials. One unusual version is the intriguing club once used by New Zealand's Maori tribesmen. Composed of nephrite jade, this club looks like a small green paddle and is said to contain spiritual powers! In a number of societies the simple club stands as a symbol of leadership and power, much like the sword in the West.

VX GAS

Developed by the British in the 1950s, this super-toxic nerve agent is good only for murder. VX gas is essentially insecticide for humans, and though the United States made tons of the stuff in the 1960s, they later decided to destroy it, along with their entire stockpile of chemical weapons. The technical name is longer than your arm, but VX essentially turns off an enzyme that controls glands and muscles—wearing them out to the point of uselessness. Tasteless and odorless, VX is actually an oily, amber-colored liquid that can be turned into a gas through extreme heat. Within a few seconds of exposure, initial symptoms (including blurred vision, headache, vomiting, and other problems) begin, and death ultimately occurs through respiratory failure.

- - - - - - - - - - - SNEAKY SABOTAGE - - - - - - - - - - -

DIVING/SCUBA "ACCIDENT"

There are a lot of logistics, training, and even math involved in a successful dive, whether you're diving for fun or as a profession. And that means there is always potential for something to go wrong—accidentally or intentionally. Such was the case when a Rhode Island dive shop owner went SCUBA diving with his wife in the British Virgin Islands… yet she didn't resurface. Ditto the Alabama newlyweds who went diving off the Great Barrier Reef on their honeymoon—but only the groom made it back alive. So be careful who you dive with, lest you wind up in deep trouble.

DIRK

A dirk is a long, straight dagger used to thrust into someone, which is extremely deadly. The word dates back to Scotland in the 1600s, and these weapons are often associated with Scottish warriors. It's a traditional weapon of the Scottish Highland soldiers, and in particular the Scottish Regiments of the British Army. Dirks were popular too among sailors back in the days of widespread pirating, since they were easy to carry while you were climbing around trying to murder people on the ship you were about to steal.

WEATHER WARFARE

While it sounds like total tin foil hat material, humankind has long attempted to manipulate the weather—and has actually made a little progress. While not something the government in any nation talks about openly, many believe the manipulation of the weather could be used for deadly intent via the creation and steering of hurricanes, earthquakes, controllable fog that uses nanotechnology, or electromagnetic weapons. The Geneva Convention now explicitly prohibits modifying the weather for military purposes, but prior to that, the United States Air Weather Service successfully "seeded" clouds above Vietnam so as to increase rainfall by around 30 percent in 1967 and 1968 (their objective was to slow the enemy). The *Washington Post* recently reported that weather control was "scientifically unjustifiable." But, then again, they *would* say that if there was a big weather-control conspiracy cover-up in the air…

BAT BOMBS

Before WWII ended, the United States was looking for creative solutions in the Pacific Theater. Since traditional Tokyo architecture at the time mainly involved wood and paper, the structures were very susceptible to fire. The United States Air Force considered dropping canisters across the city; each would contain bats attached to timed napalm explosives. The theory was that since bats like to sleep under the eaves of roofs, and in little nooks and crannies in and around buildings, they would nestle in around the city… then all the explosives would be set to detonate at the same time—resulting in presumably hundreds of simultaneous fires, and lots of enemy (and bat) death. Sounds unlikely, but according to a 2011 article in *The Atlantic*, the White House was on board, and the only reason the plan was never carried out was because advances in the atomic bomb beat it to the punch.

STUN GUN ☒ TASER

A stun gun is held against a person, who receives a direct electrical shock. A Taser is a brand-name electro-shock weapon that fires a small dart-on-a-wire that sticks into the victim; the wire then transmits electricity into the victim and stuns them. While both weapons are generally seen by both citizens and law enforcement as less-than-lethal options, they've actually killed many people, since the shock these weapons deliver can cause cardiac arrest and a number of other fatal and controversial conditions.

UMBRELLA

I t's every bit possible to dispatch some poor, unfortunate soul with the metal point of an umbrella—or by using the umbrella as a means to poison a victim. Both have happened in the real world: In 1887 in Washington DC, a man stabbed another man in the eye with an umbrella—piercing his brain and killing him! Jeez. On the poisoning front, a covert weapon known as a "Bulgarian umbrella" has a hollowed out bit at the end concealing a poison pellet. In 1978, the Bulgarian Secret Service used such an umbrella to assassinate a dissident in London. The umbrella injected the victim with ricin using compressed air. The alleged perpetrator got away with it, his… er… cover never blown.

CARBON MONOXIDE

C arbon Monoxide is a colorless, odorless gas that's simply one carbon atom and one oxygen atom. It's naturally created during phenomena such as volcanoes, forest fires, or other events where something burns; it's also generated by faulty water heaters, gas ranges, and other appliances. A little denser than air, it will kill in high concentrations. Around 170 people are killed every year by carbon monoxide, which is why carbon monoxide detectors are so important—they can help keep your family out of trouble by sounding an alarm if too much is detected. Carbon Monoxide is also found in vehicle exhaust, and its most common use as a murder weapon involves placing a victim in a confined space with an internal combustion engine (like a running car in a locked garage).

POP CULTURE **In the Alfred Hitchcock film *Strangers on a Train*, based on the Patricia Highsmith novel of the same name, one of the story's murder conspirators blithely suggests killing his father with carbon monoxide in a garage.**

- - - - - - - - - - - SLASHER MADNESS - - - - - - - - - - - -

BOLO KNIFE

A bolo is a large, machete-style knife indigenous to the Australasia region of the Indonesian archipelago and the Philippines. These murderous blades may be deadly weapons, but they're also everyday tools for peasant farmers, fishermen and other everyday folk in the region—perfect for cutting rice, cane, coconuts, and other crops. In the U.S. military, there's an old fashioned term meaning to fail a test, or to "bolo." It comes from WWII, when the US trained Filipino guerillas. The Americans tried to train locals to shoot modern firearms, but if the men failed their marksmanship tests, they were issued bolo knives instead. A bolo-wielding assassin actually tried to kill First Lady Imelda Marcos in 1972; though severely injured, she fought the guy off.

- - - - - - - - - - - - **KILLER MOVES** - - - - - - - - - - - - -

TAEKWONDO FLYING SIDEKICK

This deadly technique was originally developed to knock enemy soldiers off of horses. And such a blow could kill someone deader than a can of kimchi, either directly or as a result of the kicked person falling. The kick is a conventional front leg sidekick, whereby the martial artist rotates the hips to use the whole power of the body and strikes with the heel of the front leg (with the back leg brought up to protect the groin)—except this kick is performed in mid-air, after the fighter gets a running start. So the good news is, at least you can easily see this one coming.

- - - - - - - - - - - **SNEAKY SABOTAGE** - - - - - - - - - - - -

HYPERTHERMIA

This is the medical phrase for what happens when you overheat. The logistics around murdering someone by getting them too hot is rare, and most often murder charges involving hyperthermia come from a child being tragically left in some unfit environment—such as a hot car. But it's not just your surroundings that can cause one to boil. The drug Ecstasy (3,4-methylenedioxy-N-methlamphetamine or MDMA) can also cause the brain to overheat and kill you deader than a glow stick. Some people also get hyperthermia from a bad reaction to anesthesia, or many other medical drugs, while firefighters and other professionals who wear a lot of big, heavy personal protective equipment are also candidates for being dangerously hot (as is Bradley Cooper).

- - - - - - - - - - - - - **KILLER MOVES** - - - - - - - - - - - - -

JO STAFF

A martial arts short staff used by Japanese fighters, the traditional Jo staff is about four feet long (though its size can be tailored to best fit the specific fighter) and is made from Japanese white oak or other hardwoods. Their richness and simplicity make them not just murderous, but also quite beautiful. Some people today also make them from hickory wood that comes from Appalachia. But don't let the modest length throw you off—these sick sticks are absolute killers! In martial arts such as Aikido, Karate, and Ninjutsu, fighters learn to use this tight, mid-range weapon to defend, strike, disarm, sweep, poke, and just generally terrorize opponents.

- - - - - - - - - - - - - **THUG LIFE** - - - - - - - - - - - - -

ATTACK DOGS

L et loose the hounds of war! If you have mean dogs and you premeditatedly or accidentally set them loose on an unsuspecting person, you could totally be found guilty of murder. In 2001, a young lacrosse player was innocently walking up to her apartment with a bag of groceries when a pair of vicious dogs attacked and killed her on the spot. The dogs lived with her neighbors, a pair of lawyers who were keeping them for a member of the white supremacist Aryan Brotherhood gang while the gangster served a prison term. The couple were both charged with murder, with multiple legal findings that they knew the dogs were dangerous and failed to take precautions. As they say, when you lie down with dogs you get pleas.

- - - - - - - - - - - - FATAL FIREARMS - - - - - - - - - - - -

HK P2000

German firearms maker Heckler & Koch makes some of the finest and most highly sought after polymer handguns in the world. Introduced in 2001, the company's P2000 semi-automatic handgun was made primarily for use among law enforcement professionals and was adopted by U.S. Customs and Border Protection, the Japanese Security Police and the Swiss Border Guard. Unfortunately, they're a favorite amongst everyone—not just the good guys. A number of variants were produced, and it grew popular even with citizen shooters outside of law enforcement. But it's an expensive gun, and not everyone wants to spend that much for a high-end pistol. Until they shoot one.

- - - - - - - - - MURDER MOST STRANGE - - - - - - - - -

KAMIKAZE ATTACK

Kamikaze is a Japanese word that translates roughly into "divine" or "spirit" wind. This was the name given to special units of the Japanese military during WWII which engaged in suicide attacks across the Pacific theater. The Kamikaze used their own vehicles, typically aircraft, as killing weapons. When they ran out of ammunition or found themselves in a tight spot, they simply aimed their airplane at a vulnerable spot on an Allied ship and ran right into it like Patton Oswald through Cheetos. The kamikaze's airplane was specifically designed to inflict damage in such a way—turning the plane and pilot into a kind of guided missile, which sank dozens of enemy ships and damaged hundreds more. Proving once again that the most dangerous weapon of all is the human mind.

- - - - - - - - - - - FATAL FIREARMS - - - - - - - - - - - -

STEN GUN

Seeing service primarily in WWII, this British 9mm submachine gun was formidable, reliable, and cheap. And murderous, of course. A number of variants were made over the years, any of them killing machines. The STEN was accurate at about 100 yards and had a 32-round magazine capacity. The appeal of the STEN (whose name is an acronym of its designers) is its simplicity: some versions had as few as forty-seven parts; they were easy to make; and the British could arm insurgent forces with them without spending a great deal of money. If you look closely, you'll see STEN guns in several war movies, like *The Bridge Over the River Kwai*, *The Pianist*, and *The Eagle Has Landed*.

- - - - - - - - - - - SLASHER MADNESS - - - - - - - - - - - -

HOOK SWORD

The hook sword is a traditional Chinese martial arts weapon composed of a conventional straight sword that hooks backward at the end, with bladed crescent-moon hand-guards and a sharp, bladed hilt. They're used in pairs—one in each hand. Versatile and substantial, hook swords can be used to defend against any conventional martial arts weapon and are deadly in the hands of trained martial artists. The back of the sword is as sharp and deadly as any conventional sword, the hook on the end can be used to tear someone open and even the hilt can be used to kill via stabbing! Kung fu styles such as Northern Shaolin, Choy Li Fut, and some lineages of the Northern Praying Mantis system employ the hook sword. You'll find these flashy, deadly blades in a number of classic kung fu films including *Avenging Warriors of Shaolin* and *The Forbidden Kingdom*.

- - - - - - - - - - - - - **KILLER MOVES** - - - - - - - - - - - - - - -

KYUDO ARROWS

K yudo is traditional Japanese archery which originated among the Samurai. Using huge, elegant bows called Yumi, that have deliberately not changed much in their construction over hundreds of years, Kyudo practitioners are very much capable of killing (though it is a complex and rich art that's bigger than just the martial act). Like most martial arts, its practice is really about personal and spiritual development—and only those who stray from the path use their skills to kill. Kyudo arrows are proven deadly, though: essentially the same techniques and technology used in warfare in feudal Japan. The arrows are traditionally made from bamboo, but contemporary practitioners also use aluminum (equally deadly).

DEADLY DETAILS Unlike other Japanese specialties—like the arts of karate, jiu-jitsu, and ridiculous game shows—kyudo hasn't gained widespread popularity in the West.

BOILING OIL

This deadly thermal weapon dates back even before medieval days, when fortifications would pour boiling oil down upon invaders to dissuade them from storming a castle or city. The oil would cook opponents,

slipping into their armor and sticking to their skin to deliver a most horrible death indeed. Astonishingly, as recently as the late twentieth century, the government of Uzbekistan under President Islam Karimov (who served in 1989-1990) was accused of murdering a group of political dissidents by boiling them to death.

DEADLY DETAILS In medieval Europe, Henry VIII made boiling someone in oil an acceptable form of capital punishment; ironically, one of the people he had boiled was his cook (though the cook *had* tried to assassinate the king by poisoning his porridge).

APS UNDERWATER ASSAULT RIFLE

onventional rifles, if they fire at all underwater, aren't very accurate. But with a specially designed 5.66 bolt-style round, this Soviet-designed rifle does as advertised! The APS stands for *Avtomat Podvodny Spetsialnyy* (Special Underwater Assault Rifle), and it was adopted by the Soviet military in the mid-1970s. The APS will shoot longer and with more penetration than even a spear gun—and with a 26-round magazine capacity. It's sort of a dog when out of water; short range and with a lifespan of only a few hundred rounds, but that's not what it's for anyway.

POP CULTURE The gun is featured in the popular video game *Call of Duty: Ghosts.*

- - - - - - - - - - PERNICIOUS POISONS - - - - - - - - - -

ANTIMONY

his silvery-white element is a brittle metalloid found naturally occurring in the Earth's crust. Commercially it's used in lead batteries, and to help make fabrics and other products more flame-retardant. But poisoning someone with it will seriously curtail one's life expectancy. Though used ages ago as a medicine to treat fevers and as a laxative, ingesting antimony will likely give the victim vomiting, diarrhea, and, not surprisingly, a metallic taste in his or her mouth. The effects are similar to arsenic poisoning, and documented murders via intentional antimony poisoning are many. Polish serial killer George Chapman, known as The Borough Poisoner, murdered several women with an antimony mixture. Some speculate that Mozart may also have died of antimony poisoning.

- - - - - - - - - - - - SNEAKY SABOTAGE - - - - - - - - - - - -

"HEART ATTACK"

It is possible to murder someone just by getting them upset enough to initiate a heart attack. The forensics and legalities may be murky, but the fact is if you get someone upset enough to kill them—you're a murderer. Conspiracy theorists have lists of people a mile long who they feel have been assassinated by deliberately induced heart attacks. But the pathology reports from anyone who's had a heart attack, induced or otherwise, look similar. So who's to know?

TRUE CRIME In 2003, an arsonist who set a terrible wildfire in San Bernardino, California was charged with five counts of murder when five men had heart attacks and died after their houses burned down as a result of the arson.

- - - - - - - - - MURDER MOST STRANGE - - - - - - - - -

SOUND CANNON

The sound cannon produces a sound that's aimed in a beam and fired at enemies—causing pain and discomfort. If you're close enough to it, say 100 meters, it will cause extreme pain. Maybe even murder! It's most commonly used by oppressive governments to control crowds of unruly citizens, though it can also be mounted on an airplane to deter birds from flying in the airplane's path. A number of companies manufacture various versions of the weapon, some more dangerous than others. While marketed as "non-lethal," many versions of this technology can kill. Some tin-foil-hat types say the United States government purchased a hundred of these systems and placed them strategically around the nation in 2012 "just in case." Presumably getting ready for when the next iPhone comes out.

- - - - - - - - - - - - - **THUG LIFE** - - - - - - - - - - - - -

STONES

S toning someone to death is a form of murder that dates back to before biblical times. Also known as lapidation, reports of death by stoning have been documented in Ancient Greece; indeed, as long as there have been stones. It was often a default means of capital punishment in early civilizations. Surprisingly, stoning is still a legal means of punishment in many Middle Eastern nations, as well as in Nigeria. Even today, individual murderers worldwide look around themselves and find a rock to perform their deadly deeds.

TRUE CRIME In 2011, an Irishman murdered a friend of his by hitting him repeatedly with a stone in a drunken rage.

- - - - - - - - - - - **SLASHER MADNESS** - - - - - - - - - - -

KRIS KNIVES

K ris knives are distinctive long daggers with wavy double-edged blades, native to Indonesia. More than just a weapon, these exotic blades can also be intricate pieces of folk art— meticulously crafted and even said to contain spiritual properties! The earliest representation of these knives has dated back to a sculpture in 300 BC Vietnam, though experts claim that the kris knife truly originated in the 1360s on the island of Java. In quality kris knives, the hilt is often highly decorated and made from fine materials. The knives were also ceremonial, worn on special occasion and symbolic of power and authority.

FALLING TREE

When a tree falls and kills someone in the forest, and there are no witnesses, can anyone tell if was an accident—or murder? Between 1995 and 2007, more than 400 people in the United States alone have been killed by falling trees or limbs, usually during in a storm or just unusually high winds. And that's by accident. But it's entirely possible to kill someone by not giving them a heads-up that a giant Live Oak is falling their way. Hey, it worked for Arnold Schwarzenegger in the 1987 film *Predator*.

DEADLY DETAILS The state with the highest mortality from falling trees? Mississippi, which averages 5.27 falling tree deaths for every million people.

MCMAP RIFLE BUTT

The Marine Corps Martial Arts Program (MCMAP) is a basic hand-to-hand combat system taught to help marines engage in close quarters combat. And if The Corps uses it, you best believe t's plenty deadly! Among the system's killer techniques, which include not just empty hand but weapons training, are a number of killer rifle butt techniques. This move involves just what you'd think—swinging the butt stock of a rifle (the end that snugs up against your shoulder) into the head of your opponent. Performed vertically or horizontally and with a few variations, the Marine puts his or her whole bodyweight behind the strike by timing step and hip rotation with the hit. The result? Killing someone faster than a bottle of Jack Daniels at a family reunion.

- - - - - - - - - - PERNICIOUS POISONS - - - - - - - - - - -

AZALEAS

The azalea is a flowering shrub whose beauty and hardiness have made them one of the most popular decorative plants in the world. But they're also downright deadly. Azaleas contain andromedotoxins, which damage human cells, in their leaves and nectar. In fact, their murderous potential is so ominous that to receive a bouquet of azaleas in a black vase was once a well-known death threat. Azaleas contain the same type of toxin as rhododenrons (the two flowers are very similar). You have to consume quite a bit of an azalea to actually die; maybe .2 percent of the person's body weight. But beware: children and pets are especially susceptible, as eating relatively little can be deadly.

- - - - - - - - - - - - - THUG LIFE - - - - - - - - - - - - -

MACE OR FLAIL

Popular in Europe during the Middle Ages (fifth through fifteenth centuries), a mace is a stick with a metal ball at one end used for striking. Similarly, a "morning star" is a mace with raised spikes on the metal ball. And even creepier, a "flail" is a stick with a metal spiked ball that is attached with a metal chain. Originally used for threshing, these tools all evolved into handheld weapons popular with Medieval knights—infantry and cavalry alike. Some were huge, taking two hands to wield, and others were relatively light, one-handed affairs. See them in *Braveheart*, *A Knight's Tale*, *The Princess Bride*, and American Black Friday shopping mobs.

- - - - - - - - - MURDER MOST STRANGE - - - - - - - - -

WILD ANIMALS

S etting wild animals upon someone else takes a bit of logistical planning, but it's a proven form of murder. The ancient Romans were actually quite good at it. In the Roman Colosseum, a major event was the fighting of the *bestiari*. Just as gladiators fought other men, the bestiaries fought wild animals. Usually they were poor slaves, and didn't stand much of a chance. Many simply killed themselves before the fight. When a Roman soldier deserted the army and was caught, his sentence was often *damnatio ad bestias*—death by beast. The subject would be at a disadvantage, such as tied down or unarmed completely, and would be mauled outright. It would be hard to set up such a scene and wonder if you'd not become a wild animal yourself.

DEADLY DETAILS Being trampled by elephants was a common *damnatio ad bestias*.

- - - - - - - - - - - SLASHER MADNESS - - - - - - - - - - -

NAGINATA

T hese deadly weapons from feudal Japan are sheer murder-on-a-stick! Much like a halberd (though with a thicker pole and a thinner blade), the naginata is composed of a curved blade on the end of a long oaken staff. The weapon could be as long as nine feet depending on the fighter, and took a significant amount of training to use effectively. Naginatas served a number of purposes including defense against mounted cavalry and by Japanese housewives for home defense (and presumably, against adulterous husbands). The art of fighting with these esoteric weapons was passed down across several generations and is still practiced today. The martial arts of Jikishinkage-ryu, Tendo-ryu, and even some schools of ninjutsu, all practice the deadly fighting techniques of the naginata.

- - - - - - - - - - - - - - THUG LIFE - - - - - - - - - - - - - -

ROLL OF COINS

Whether pennies or quarters, a roll of coins is a hard and heavy object that's every bit capable of being used as a murder weapon. They can be tucked inside the palm while punching the victim, brass knuckle style, or placed in a sock or other cloth and swung at the victim. Of course, now that U.S. coins are purely "fiat currency" based on and containing few precious metals at all, today's lightweight roll of coins might not be the lethal weapon it once was.

POP CULTURE In the 1974 Charles Bronson film *Death Wish*, a vigilante uses a roll of coins to put somebody's lights out.

- - - - - - - - - - - SNEAKY SABOTAGE - - - - - - - - - - -

TAR PIT

It's absolutely possible to murder someone by finding a tar pit, and then throwing your victim into it. These smelly, sticky pools of asphalt occur naturally, although there are only a handful around the world, in places such as California, Texas, Venezuela, and Russia. The most famous is the La Brea Tar Pits in Los Angeles (La Brea means "tar" in Spanish), which is tens of thousands of years old. Tar pits are notorious for trapping animals accidentally, and have also been used to hide murder evidence or dispose of the odd unfortunate victim. In 2011, homicide investigators dove into the La Brea pit for the first time in history to retrieve a murder weapon that had been thrown into it.

- - - - - - - - - - - **PERNICIOUS POISONS** - - - - - - - - - - -
DEPLETED URANIUM

Depleted uranium is just uranium that's got a bit less U-235, usually as a byproduct of making enriched uranium for another purpose (like building a nuclear reactor). But this toxic metal can also be used for outright murder. The military uses depleted uranium for a number of applications; the most controversial is probably ammunition. As it turns out, depleted uranium can be mixed with small amounts of other metals to make super-effective armor-piercing rounds that can punch through thick armor. It's used because of its metallurgical reaction upon impacting a target, not because of its radioactive properties. An estimated 1,000 murderous tons of depleted uranium was sprayed across Iraq by Allied forces in 2003 alone.

- - - - - - - - - - - **KILLER MOVES** - - - - - - - - - - -
HOOK KNIVES

A hook knife is exactly what it sounds like: a small, handheld knife with a blade that's shaped like a hook (all along the same plane but shaped like a "J"). Utility knives typically used to clean game animals, open packages, or perform other types of manual labor, they could also be used for murder! Unlike the huge, unwieldy hook swords of the martial arts world, the hook knife is a pocket tool—often employed by paramedics and firefighters to cut people out of seatbelts and perform other tactical duties.

DEADLY DETAILS Also called a "hook knife" is an old fashioned whittling tool where the blade is curled sideways as if wrapped around something. These are also potentially deadly … when it comes to killing time.

- - - - - - - - - **MURDER MOST STRANGE** - - - - - - - - -
RUSSIAN ROULETTE

Some disturbed people make a game out of murder. For example, in "Russian Roulette," a player loads a single round into a revolver and spins the chamber, snapping the gun closed at random and cocking it. He then puts it up to his head and pulls the trigger, with around a sixteen percent chance of ending it all on any given spin. Who would play such a terrible game? A crazy person. And who would force someone to play? A killer, that's who. Recently a Richardson, Texas man was charged with manslaughter after shooting and killing his friend in a game of Russian roulette (they were taking turns pulling the trigger on each other in a hotel parking lot).

DEADLY DETAILS Other deadly "games" include automobile "chicken," in which two cars head straight on and the one who turn away first loses, or forcing prisoners to fight each other to the deatl gladiator style (you know, sort of like a Girl Scout cookie sales contest).

POTS *AND* PANS

They say that most parties, no matter where they begin, end up with guests congregating in the kitchen. The same can hold true for murder! And there's more to be wary of in the kitchen than only the knives. Big, heavy, and always at hand, your average household pots and pans can also become deadly weapons before you know it. Be especially careful around the frying pans; in 2014, a man in Queens killed his brother with a frying pan, and in 1980, a Florida woman beat her husband to death with a skillet. So stop and think twice next time before you criticize someone's béchamel sauce.

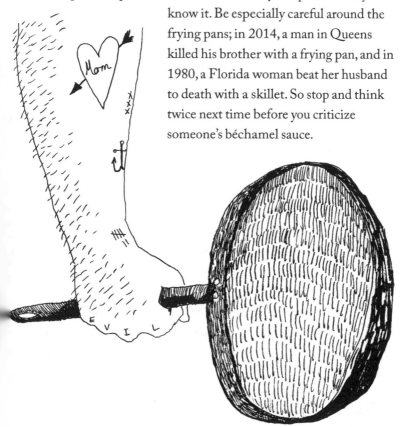

BENT BARREL STURMGEWEHR

A product of Nazi Germany, the Sturmgewehr ("assault rifle") 44, also known as the StG 44, came in this unusual variant. The gun actually had a bent barrel! Yup, through the addition of a barrel attachment known as a Krummlauf (Gesundeit!), the gun was made to shoot around corners more effectively. With a complicated scope that works a bit like a periscope, these guns were used by both infantry and tank personnel. It was a murderous innovation, and these barrel attachments came in a variety of angles. But they weren't flawless. Bullets tended to fragment on the way out of the gun because of the mechanical stresses involved. And after a few hundred rounds, they were useless.

- - - - - - - - - - - SLASHER MADNESS - - - - - - - - - - - -

STAKE

It's entirely possible to murder someone with a stake through the heart (or too many steaks and a heart condition. *Ba-dum-ching*!) An old legend says the only true way to kill a vampire is to drive a wooden stake through its heart. Indeed, the bodies of more than 100 Bulgarian "vampires" from the Middle Ages were recently unearthed with iron stakes protruding from their chests. These poor souls weren't blood-sucking monsters, but merely aristocrats or other people whom the townsfolk just didn't like very much. In modern times, the equivalent of hammering an iron stake into someone's chest is not "liking" their Facebook post.

206

CONSTITUTION ARMS PALM PISTOL

C onstitution's Palm Pistol is a single-shot belly gun that looks a bit like an elongated black egg and fits into the palm of your hand. This sneaky little .38-caliber firearm looks like it came from outer space, but is murderously easy to use. It can be fired ambidextrously, and the barrel simply juts out from between your fingers with the stock fitting right in your hand. Usually fired with the thumb, it can even be fitted with a laser sight. This gun has gained a lot of buzz because it can be fired by people with arthritic hands, who might not be able to operate a conventional firearm. So when your cranky neighbor says "get off my lawn," you'd better do it!

- - - - - - - - - - - SNEAKY SABOTAGE - - - - - - - - - - -

BIKING "ACCIDENT"

M ore than 60,000 cyclists fall and hit their heads each year; hundreds of cyclists die on the road. It's a challenging and rewarding sport—but also a dangerous one. That's why it would be so easy to cause an "accident" that wasn't accidental at all. If the victim doesn't make it, and there were no witnesses, who's to say the victim didn't simply fall? Theo van Gogh, great-nephew to painter Vincent van Gogh, was murdered while riding his bike in Amsterdam—though he was shot eight times, so nobody really thought it was an accident.

DEADLY DETAILS Negligent automobile drivers are often charged with murder if they kill a cyclist on the road.

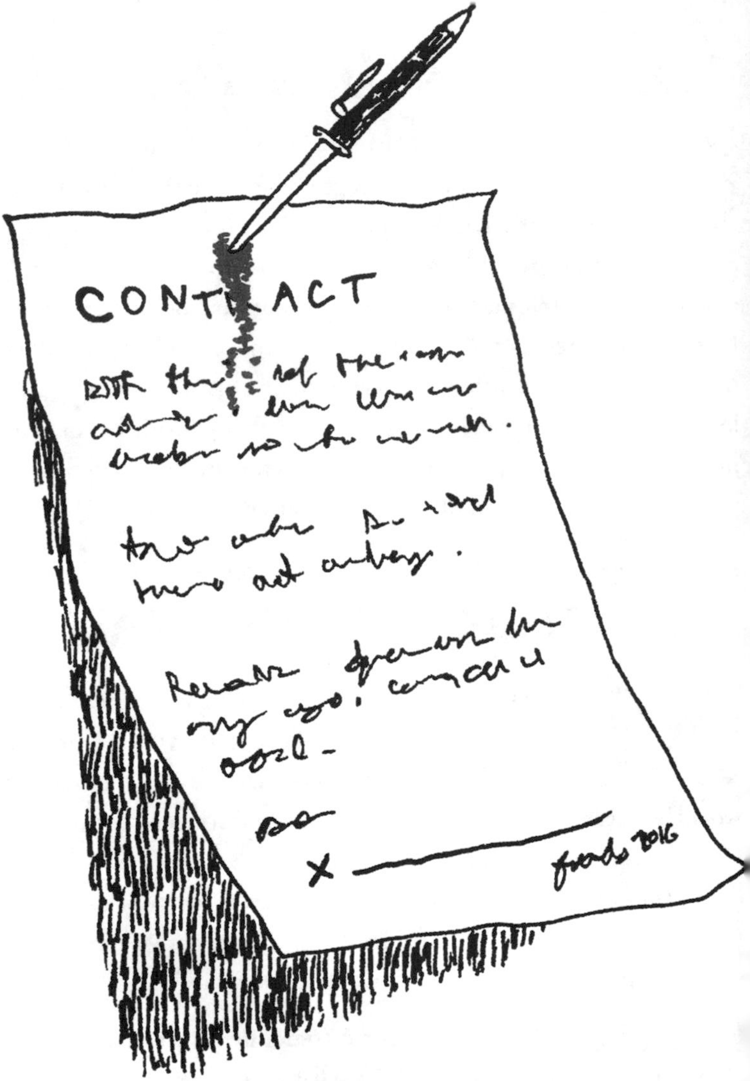
CONTRACT

BALLPOINT
PEN KNIFE

Just as the name implies, a ballpoint penknife looks like a regular writing utensil on the outside, but conceals a sharp blade. They were originally handmade and used in early attempts at spy craft (or as self-defense weapons), but today they are mass-produced and relatively inexpensive—which makes them dangerously perfect for murder. In 1996, a barmaid and former model in the United Kingdom murdered her fiancé with a pen knife by stabbing him more than 30 times during an argument in the man's car.

DEADLY DETAILS The phrase "pen knife" predates these hidden blades by some time. Originally, a "pen knife" was any small but sharp knife that was kept on hand at your desk to sharpen writing quills before the days of refillable or disposable pens, back before texting and emojis.

BROKEN MIRROR

Murdering someone with a broken mirror will not only get you seven years bad luck—but also life in prison! Like any broken glass, a hunk of broken mirror can be deadly sharp. People are murdered with mirrors all the time. In 2014, a Hackensack, New Jersey man was arguing with his girlfriend when another man intervened on the girl's behalf. For the Good Samaritan's troubles, the boyfriend stabbed him repeatedly with a piece of broken mirror, and he eventually died from the wounds. Some superstitious people say that you can reverse the seven years of bad luck by placing the pieces of the broken mirror in a bag and burying them (without killing anyone). Others say you can reverse the bad luck by leaving New Jersey.

IRON MAIDEN

No, not the super-awesome music group; here we're talking about the torture device after which the band was named. A terribly murderous-looking machine, the iron maiden is basically a sarcophagus with metal spikes facing inside. When closed, the tortured soul within is poked all over his or her body. Most people think this contraption dates back to medieval days and the Spanish Inquisition, but nobody has come up with one predating 1800 or so. In fact, some say that it was just a gimmick created in the 1700s or 1800s for entertainment, and was never really used to torture people— unlike the heavy metal band of the same name. But if you see one, take the band's advice and run to the hills!

HYDROFLUORIC ACID

T his is basically just hydrogen fluoride, a super-corrosive chemical gas, dissolved in water. It has a number of useful commercial applications, particularly in manufacturing and petrochemicals, but unless you just have to—or you're looking to murder someone in a most hideous way—stay well clear of the stuff. When the human body comes into contact with hydrofluoric acid, the acid passes right through the skin and starts tearing through cells in the body. Whatever it touches will never work right again; breathing the stuff damages your lungs, and even if you survive the exposure, you'll likely have mucho problems. Just a gram-and-a-half of this stuff will be the end of someone.

DEADLY DETAILS **When not serving as a diabolical evil weapon, hydrofluoric acid is used to make high-octane gasoline, electrical components and fluorescent light bulbs.**

- - - - - - - - - - - - - KILLER MOVES - - - - - - - - - - - - -

KUBOTAN:
THE KILLER KEYCHAIN

A kubotan is a cylindrical metal handheld spike designed for self-defense, but which could very easily be used for murder. It's typically held within a closed fist and used to as a blunt-force weapon to strike the head, torso, and other squishy bits of the human anatomy. Designed by Japanese karate master Takayuki Kubota, the weapon was first introduced to police officers in Los Angeles. When it came out nobody really knew what it was; it just looked like a harmless keychain (in fact, except when carried by law enforcement officers, they are almost always designed as keychains, so they'll always be handy). These days it's easily recognizable as a makeshift weapon and even illegal in some places. So don't carry them where it's illegal; if it's confiscated, there go your keys!

- - - - - - - - - - - **SLASHER MADNESS** - - - - - - - - - - - -

MEAT THERMOMETER

That's right, the same thermometer that works so hard to keep your pork roast honest can also work hard at murder! There's a scene in the 1998 film *The Perfect Murder* (a solid remake of Alfred Hitchcock's *Dial M for Murder*), where Gwyneth Paltrow's character stabs her would-be assassin in the neck with a meat thermometer. It's happened in real life, too. In 2010, a Los Angeles moviegoer was also stabbed in the neck after asking a fellow patron to turn off a mobile phone during the movie. The victim was lucky to have lived through the attack. Who brings a meat thermometer to the movies anyway? The victim's internal temperature was not disclosed at the time of the attack.

- - - - - - - - - - - **FATAL FIREARMS** - - - - - - - - - - - -

NAZI BELT BUCKLE PISTOL

Leave it to the Nazis to turn even a plain old belt buckle into an evil killing machine. These rare firearms looked like your run-of-the-mill Nazi belt buckle (with an angry psycho eagle and a swastika design), but the front plate swung upward to turn this ordinary buckle into instant Nazi Death Crotch. These guns were issued to high-ranking officers in case of their capture (though it didn't seem to do them much good in the end). Chambered in either .22LR or 7.65, the gun held four shots with small buttons on the side of the buckle serving as the triggers. Fewer than ten of these rare WWII relics are known to exist.

BLOODBORNE PATHOGENS

A bloodborne pathogen is any infectious micro-organism that can transmit a disease through the blood. It's possible to murder someone by exposing them to bloodborne pathogens, including potentially deadly diseases like Human Immunodeficiency Virus (HIV) or hepatitis. It's not unheard of for people who knowingly spread diseases such as HIV/AIDS to another to be charged with murder, whether as serving as a sexual partner or by using needles or other implements. It's also possible to transmit a disease through a blood transfusion.

DEADLY DETAILS Pathogens spread by insects, such as malaria, are called vector-borne pathogens.

FEAR

S cientists have proven that you truly can scare somebody to death. In a fight-or-flight situation, your body dumps adrenaline into your system. And at super-high levels, adrenaline can be toxic and lead to heart failure. In 2009, a North Carolina woman was home alone when a man who'd tried to rob a bank broke into her home to elude police. She was so frightened, the poor old dear died on the spot. And in 2013, a Brooklyn man with eight children was scared to death by police officers who busted into his house at 5:30am (they were breaking down doors looking for a robbery suspect; unfortunately for everyone, this wasn't the guy). So the next time you think about scaring a friend with a practical joke, think twice: you wouldn't want it to be your last laugh together.

- - - - - - - - - - - - - **KILLER MOVES** - - - - - - - - - - - - -

KOREAN DANG PA

The Dang Pa is a traditional Korean martial arts weapon that's basically a long, three-pronged spear. And it's absolutely capable of murder. The dang pa is composed of a hard wood, but the spiked base and metal prongs on the end are covered in heavy metal to better withstand impact. The side prongs are angled outward and the center prong is longer than the others—to keep the weapon from being stuck in an unfortunate victim. There aren't very many schools who still teach dang pa fighting techniques, even within traditional Korean martial arts schools, so rare is the man or woman who can truly use one for combat applications. So that would narrow down your list of suspects.

- - - - - - - - - **MURDER MOST STRANGE** - - - - - - - - -

BROKEN HEART

You hear about it all the time; someone loses a spouse, and then dies shortly thereafter. So it is possible to kill someone by murdering their mate? Scientists say it is. Studies have shown that a person's risk of heart attack and stroke are higher after losing a loved one—especially the first month after the fact. Some medical experts are calling this "broken heart syndrome." In addition to sheer physiological stress, people who rely on lifesaving medications may simply forget to take them while grieving. So at the end of the day, if someone were the murdering sort, it could be entirely possible to kill someone by killing their spouse. Love really does hurt.

- - - - - - - - - - - - - THUG LIFE - - - - - - - - - - - - - -

MOLOTOV COCKTAIL

A Molotov Cocktail is a homemade fire bomb typically composed of flammable liquid inside a glass bottle, with a rag stuffed in the top that's lit afire. When thrown at something, the bottle breaks and covers the target in flames. It was first used in the Spanish Civil War as an anti-tank weapon—originally containing tar so that the fire would stick to the tanks and do more damage. Its name comes from a WWII-era Soviet military leader named Vyacheslav Molotov. When the Soviets invaded Finland, they used these "Molotov Cocktails" to welcome invading Soviet tank regiments.

- - - - - - - - - - - - KILLER MOVES - - - - - - - - - - - - -

SPEAR HAND ATTACK

A spear hand is a traditional martial arts technique found in Japanese karate, Korean taekwondo, and some forms of Chinese kung fu. The technique consists of holding one's hand flat like a blade and thrusting it forward into a soft target such as the opponent's throat. The result can be deadly! The technique could theoretically collapse the airway resulting in suffocation, or be used in other devious ways to kill. But the person who uses this technique correctly is a martial arts expert. It would take years of conditioning the hand and a lot of precision to be able to be able to perform the spear hand technique to its fullest murderous potential. But the beauty of this deadly technique? It's always handy should you need it.

- - - - - - - - - **MURDER MOST STRANGE** - - - - - - - - -

"WEAPONIZED" DISEASE

It is possible to use intentional exposure to any deadly disease as a way to kill. "Weaponized" diseases such as smallpox, pneumonic plague, cholera, *E. coli*, Lassa fever, typhoid, and other sicknesses have all been used as biological weapons to kill both individuals and opposing armies. In one elaborate and highly sensational murder case in 1925, a millionaire orphan died of typhoid fever, leaving his entire vast fortune to his lawyer. The lawyer was accused of having rewritten the man's will to his own benefit, then conspiring with a doctor to give the victim typhoid germs for his deadly plot. It's been proven that both the United States and Russia have developed a "weaponized" strain of Anthrax (Page 50), which has a mortality rate of over 95 percent if not treated within 48 hours after initial symptoms!

DEADLY DETAILS Because bioweapons are so potentially harmful, 165 countries signed an agreement in 1972 outlawing the production and use of these murderous weapons.

DUELING PISTOLS

At one point in history, dueling was a socially acceptable and legal way for two parties to settle a dispute. The point was restoring honor after a perceived slight. But plenty of people were killed. Dueling was originally done with swords, and later with pistols. Dueling pistols were even sold in sets, quite intricate and ornate by today's standards, and are collectables today. Dueling in the United States was outlawed in the mid-1800s, and pretty much stopped altogether after the War Between the States. Murder via "Dueling Banjos" has yet to be documented.

TRUE CRIME **One of the most famous American duels went down in 1804 when Vice President Aaron Burr—that's right, the actual sitting Vice President of the United States—shot and mortally wounded founding father Alexander Hamilton. Tension between the two had been mounting for years, and Hamilton's trash talk in the press as Burr ran for office pushed things over the top. Burr was indicted for murder but later acquitted, probably because he helped run the country.**

MOSSBERG 500 CHAINSAW ZMB EDITION

The Mossberg 500 Chainsaw isn't a chainsaw at all, but a six-round capacity 12-gauge pump shotgun, perfect for the upcoming zombie apocalypse—or just plain old murder. It's like any other pistol-grip tactical-style shotgun, except that it's meant to be fired from the hip and has a large, square chainsaw-style handle mounted on the top. The Mossberg Chainsaw looks like something out of the *Terminator* or *Mad Max* films. Plenty capable of murdering a man or woman, the gun's actual efficacy in dispatching the undead remains untested. For now.

DEADLY DETAILS The gun comes in a special "Zombie" edition, with a custom-creepy ZMB logo on the side.

SELF-CLEANING OVENS

Killing someone in the kitchen can mean more than just whipping up a poison pie. Sometimes all it takes is to turn the oven onto its "self-cleaning" mode. Self-cleaning ovens heat themselves to extreme temperatures—burning up any food spilled inside the oven, and cleaning it thermally. The problem is that ovens coated in Polytetrafluoroethylene (PTFE) can create potentially deadly fumes; the PTFE is said to break down at high temperatures creating toxic particulates that can cause cancer and present symptoms similar to the nerve gas phosphine, a chemical weapon used during WWII. Self-cleaning ovens have caused the deaths of many pet birds, such as parrots (which are extremely vulnerable to these toxins). All that said, the risk of PTFE-related illness would be worth it for some if they could avoid their filled crepes from breaking apart.

- - - - - - - - - - - - - - THUG LIFE - - - - - - - - - - - - - -

LEAD PIPE

A lead pipe is an iconic thug's weapon made famous by the murder mystery board game *Clue* (*Cluedo* in the UK), though fewer and fewer murderers would know where to get one. Lead pipe has been manufactured since ancient Rome, though it might have done more killing by poisoning the water than blunt force. Before people realized how unhealthy it was to ingest even tiny amounts of lead, a lot of pipes were made from lead because it's a very malleable heavy metal and easy to form. But get hit in the head with a lead pipe, and it won't feel malleable—it will feel fatal.

DEADLY DETAILS Lead is extremely heavy; they're why things like fishing weights are often made of lead. A cubic foot of lead weighs over 700 pounds!

- - - - - - - - - - - - FATAL FIREARMS - - - - - - - - - - - -

MARLIN MODEL 60

T he Model 60 is a semi-automatic rifle chambered to fire .22LR rimfire ammo. Designed in 1960, over 11 million of these inexpensive rifles have been sold in past decades. So one of them was bound to end up in the hands of a murderer. Cheap, reliable, and great for shooting small game or just plinking at the range, this rifle was branded and sold under department store labels such as Montgomery Ward and JC Penney. This is often thought of as a beginner's gun. It holds between fourteen and eighteen rounds of potential murder, depending on when it was made. Rumors that the company also made a Marlon Brando Model 60 that could hold several dozen rounds of Mallomars could not be substantiated.

- - - - - - - - - MURDER MOST STRANGE - - - - - - - - -

METAL POISONING

P oisoning someone with toxic metals, such as thallium, copper, magnesium, or lead can kill them deader than a coffee can full of nails. The human body can process a certain amount of metal. But once that threshold is hit, the damage begins. Symptoms can include nausea, headaches, digestive problems, hair loss, and—not surprisingly—a metallic taste in the victim's mouth. In 2011, a New Jersey chemist poisoned her husband with thallium to avoid finalizing their divorce; she'd stolen the material from the lab where she worked.

- - - - - - - - - - SLASHER MADNESS - - - - - - - - - -

SABRE

T he sabre is a long, curved sword with a single straight blade and sturdy hand guard across the hilt. They served as a popular military weapon among European cavalrymen in the 1800s, and have seen more than their share of murder. Dating back to at least the 1600s, the word comes from an ancient Turkic word meaning "to cut." The popularity of the sabre as a military implement reached its height during the Napoleonic Wars (1803-1815)—after that, though, advancements in long guns meant there wasn't much advantage to having a sword dangling around your waist in battle.

DEADLY DETAILS To this day in the United States, a ceremonial sabre is part of the official dress uniform for all branches of the military.

- - - - - - - - - - PERNICIOUS POISONS - - - - - - - - - - -

PARAKEET POOP

That's right. Millions of people keep pet parakeets, love them like family, and never get sick. But if the bird is ill, and the cage isn't as clean as it should be, its owners could become sick. Or even dead! After sitting for a while, the poop that collects in the bottom of a parakeet's cage will begin to aerosolize, and those around the bird will breathe in the particulates or accidentally ingest them in their food or drink (ew). So in this manner, potentially life-threatening diseases such as West Nile virus, encephalitis, influenza, or salmonellosis could be unknowingly transmitted to those around the bird—potentially with deadly consequences. So you had better teach the bird to say: "I want a lawyer!"

TRUE SADNESS In what is arguably the saddest thing ever written in the history of Florida or parakeets, a Palm Harbor man passed away 1991 the day after his pet parakeet, Pretty Boy, died.

SOCKS

That's right—just plain, old everyday socks. They can be stuffed in someone's mouth until the victim chokes to death or used to strangle a person (though it would have to be sort of a long sock). In 2007, a young man claimed that he and a lady friend had been using socks during rough sex when he inadvertently strangled her (maybe so, but he can't blame the socks for his next move, which was to torch her house and run; he was eventually caught and convicted of manslaughter and arson). And in Lubbock, Texas, a man was strangled to death with a sock during a beer run when the victim refused to pay for the murderer's beer.

KILLING BY CONFINEMENT

You can absolutely murder somebody by locking them inside a small space and leaving them there to die of suffocation, hunger, or thirst. Murderers have been known to lock people inside of large safes, basements, crates, closets, tanks, containers, and other strange places. In one especially baffling case, a code-breaking British spy was found dead inside of a huge gym bag with a padlock on it. Scotland Yard detectives determined that he could very well have locked himself inside of the bag—but, then again, that's what a government official might say when commenting on the high-profile and unorthodox death of a spy, eh?

- - - - - - - - - - - - - KILLER MOVES - - - - - - - - - - - - -

HAMMER-FIST STRIKE

A hammer-fist is when you make a fist, but rather than hit someone with your knuckles, you use the meaty bottom part of your hand (so that your fingers are stacked vertically and out of the way). It's a killer technique. In addition to the murderous possibility of knocking someone out and having them cause irreparable brain damage hitting the pavement, using a hammer-fist once your victim is down can cause life-ending brain trauma. You'll see professional fighters in the UFC and other hardcore MMA contestants throwing hammer-fists to an opponent's head once they're down because it's just devastating. Once this starts and the downed man can no longer defend himself, often the ref calls the fight for the safety of the defeated.

HARD CANDIES

More than just potential choking hazards, sometimes hard candies can be even more lethal. For instance, Jolly Ranchers are a super-popular and yummy fruit-flavored candy that dates back to 1949. But in the hands of a prison thug, these candies can cut you dead! That's right: Crafty inmates in prison have been known to melt the candies together and then shape them into sharp pointed shanks that harden as they cool. It takes about five Jolly Ranchers to make a dangerous and sturdy shank out of once harmless candy. And, if these prison thugs don't mind the taste of blood, they could eat the evidence later! Once prisoners figured this out, just about everybody in cellblocks around the world lost their hard candy privileges.

- - - - - - - - - - - - SNEAKY SABOTAGE - - - - - - - - - - - -

"FAULTY" ELEVATOR

Talk about nightmares! It's entirely possible to murder someone by sabotaging an elevator just before they get on it. But sabotaging an elevator is tough (thank goodness!); most have six or so cables supporting the carriage, and each supports 150 percent of the unit's weight rating. It's more likely that murderers could trick their victims into believing that an elevator had arrived—only, instead of an actual elevator, it's just an empty shaft. So if the victim isn't paying attention, he or she is going down for the count. Broken elevators are one of the most common stressful dreams Americans have between the ages of 20–40, and can represent frustration among those striving towards a goal.

BOX CUTTER

A box cutter is a tool, typically made of a sturdy metal or plastic, with a handle that houses a replaceable flat razor, making precision cutting easy. And because so many people get packages every day, they're found at just about every office, household, school, hospital, restaurant, and factory. Sadly, however, people are murdered every year with these innocuous tools. While many people simply need to open boxes, some people who aren't right in the head have also used box cutters to open their fellow man. Like many other everyday items, box cutters can help someone either get things done—or get into serious trouble.

POP CULTURE In the popular AMC television series *Breaking Bad*, one of Walter White's coworkers is nonchalantly killed with a box cutter to enforce discipline in the organization.

- - - - - - - - - - - FATAL FIREARMS - - - - - - - - - - -

NORTH AMERICAN ARMS .22

NA Arms is a Utah-based company that makes teeny-tiny pistols and revolvers. Its wee .22s are made of stainless steel, and resemble the old-time pocket revolvers gamblers used to carry on their person during the 1800s. These guns may be small, but they pack a deadly punch! They are available in a variety of .22 variants, and are super-popular self-defense weapons because they're just so easy to carry. You don't even need a holster—just stick them in your pocket.

One model even has a folding handle, much like a pocketknife. Robert Duvall carried one in *Assassination Tango*, and you can see Val Kilmer sporting an NAA mini-revolver in *Kiss, Kiss, Bang, Bang*. 'Murica!

BENZODIAZEPINE

This psychoactive drug can really mellow you out—or kill you, if placed in the wrong hands. Primarily known as tranquilizers, there are many different types of benzodiazepines that successfully aid in a number of medical conditions such as anxiety, insomnia, and seizures. These drugs work by enhancing the effect of the major inhibitory neurotransmitter in the body's central nervous system. It's possible to murder someone via an "accidental" overdose of benzodiazepines, but what really makes them deadly is that these drugs become super-toxic when mixed with liquor and other drugs or anti-depressants. Worst. Trip. Ever.

DEADLY DETAILS **The brand name drugs Valium and Xanax are both benzodiazepines.**

- - - - - - - - - - - - - **KILLER MOVES** - - - - - - - - - - - - -

HEAD-BUTT

A favorite fighting technique among British and European football hooligans, a head-butt involves using the hardest, thick part of the cranium to strike someone in the nose or other soft target area. And it can totally kill. A Nigerian man killed his neighbor in 2014 with a head-butt after the neighbor allegedly spanked the man's child. In 2010, a British couple was waiting for a taxi when two thugs came out of nowhere, one of them head-butting the man to death. And in 2007, a Georgia man died after getting head-butted by an armless acquaintance during a fight over a woman (though his cause of death was ultimately attributed to a heart attack). Come on, humanity—start using your head for what it was intended.

- - - - - - - - - MURDER MOST STRANGE - - - - - - - - -

HUGE BREASTS

Talk about killer cleavage! It's completely possible for a woman to kill someone by smothering a victim to death with her ample bosom. In 2013, a Washington State woman was accused of smothering and killing her boyfriend with her huge breasts. Apparently, she and her boyfriend had been drinking, smoking dope, and fighting. The fighting part would prove fatal to him, since she outweighed him by around twenty pounds. Witnesses on the scene described finding her passed out on top of him, and the poor man unresponsive to CPR, with clumps of her hair in his hands. (Reports of a smile on his face could not be confirmed.) She was charged with second-degree manslaughter. And while a personal tragedy for those involved, the incident teaches humanity a valuable lesson: try to be kind to your bosom buddies.

- - - - - - - - - - - - - THUG LIFE - - - - - - - - - - - - -

GAMING CONSOLE

Everybody knows that video games aren't great for you, what with all that sitting around the living room and such. But did you know they could also be used as murder weapons? These gaming consoles are hard plastic boxes about the size of a textbook, and hefty enough to be deadly. Some argue that the most murderous potential of these games isn't in the box but in the brain—desensitizing players to crime and violence, and blurring the lines between online and real-life behavior. In fact, people have even killed for the gaming systems themselves. In 2004, in what became known as the "Xbox Murders," a group of men broke into a home and bludgeoned six residents with baseball bats to get a gaming console and some other property the group's leader claimed was his. Game over.

TRUE CRIME   **In 2013, a Florida man allegedly killed his girlfriend by beating her to death with an Xbox and then stabbing her, later claiming that she was controlling his mind against his will, and that he had to kill her because her astrological sign was Taurus and it was the only way to free his soul (the poor man was clearly two tacos short of the full combination platter).**

- - - - - - - - - - - SLASHER MADNESS - - - - - - - - - - -

SPOON

It's not your typical bladed weapon, but death-by-spoon is actually a thing. In 1980, an inmate at Florida State Prison killed a guard with a spoon as he was being escorted to the shower. And in 2003, a British man was acquitted on charges of killing someone with a dessert spoon (no word on whether it had been kept in its proper place in the setting, which is directly above the plate). Jesse Eisenburg's character in the movie *American Ultra* kills a man with a spoon—because he's just that deadly. So when you have strangers over, watch your silverware; not because it's silver but because it's killer!

BOTULINUM

Botulinum is a wicked little protein created by a bacterium called *Clostridium botulinum*. And it just may be the most lethal toxin known to mankind. A deadly neurotoxin, small amounts of botulinum cause botulism, which paralyzes victims, promotes all kinds of diseases, and can be fatal. The deployment of an aerosol or foodborne botulinum toxin has even been reviewed as a potential terrorist bioweapon because it's easy to make and transport, difficult to detect, and just plain deadly. In the 1931 novel *Malice Aforethought*, the murderer spreads botulism on his victim's sandwiches. Yum!

DEADLY DETAILS The cosmetic injection Botox is composed of Botulinum Toxin A, so don't get stuck in the wrong place.

WELL POISONING

We all need water. So the person who would poison a water well is truly a murderer indeed. In times of war dating back to the Assyrians, poisoning a well was proven an effective tactic—either offensively to destabilize a defender or defensively when denying water to an invading army. One ancient tactic was simply to throw rotting corpses into the well. The practice continues to this day, and not just as a military tactic. In 2009, Filipino political activists poisoned a local water supply; and just a few years before, somebody laced a Danish reservoir with strychnine. In 2002,

Al Qaeda terrorists were even caught planning to contaminate the water supply in Paris. But you're better off drinking the wine anyway.

THROWING BUFFALO PUNCH

The "throwing buffalo" punch—which is actually a thing—is a powerful technique from the Eastern Thai martial art of Muay Korat. Muay Korat is a subset of Muay Boran, which translates to "ancient boxing." It is the progenitor of Muay Thai boxing and the contemporary Thai boxing styles we see today. And any of these martial arts could be used to kill. The "throwing buffalo" punch is a technique said to be so powerful that it could knock out a buffalo! Not many know how to do it these days, as teachers of ancient Siamese combat techniques are pretty rare. But that's just as well; there aren't many buffalo left to punch, either. Poor buffalo.

THE CHALK OF FAME

There's just nothing pleasant about any kind of murder. But in our estimation, these 10 murder methods strike us as especially murder-tastic.

ENTOMBING or BURYING ALIVE (P. 16)

You can't move. You can't breathe. You probably can't scratch, well, anything. What a way to depart this mortal plane.

CURSES and MAGIC SPELLS (P. 110)

The last thing you'd think was how such a thing was truly possible after all… (Cue dramatic '40s organ music from horror radio show.)

AIRPLANE "MALFUNCTION" (P. 127)

In the gravity of the situation, you'd wonder if those who wished to do you harm were actually capable of taking it this far.

NAPALM (P. 163)

Somebody made FIRE THAT STICKS TO YOU. Repeat: FIRE THAT STICKS TO YOU! Thanks a lot, science.

THE "V" OF DEATH (P. 164)

Not good for anyone involved, attempted murder by this means takes "toxic relationship" to a new level.

"FAULTY" ELEVATOR (P. 225)

It's that nightmare you had, only it's real—and that button won't help no matter how many times you press it.

HUGE BREASTS (P. 228)

Beware of the twins, and not just in "The Shining." We're all just areolae-n-the-hay away from meeting our bust rewards.

INDEX

235

---------- **ABOUT THE AUTHOR** ----------

WILLIAM DYLAN POWELL writes dark, and
often funny, stories about crime. An active member of the Mystery Writers
of America, his crime fiction has been featured in *Ellery Queen's Mystery
Magazine, Alfred Hitchcock's Mystery Magazine, Needle: A Magazine of Noir*
and other shady publications. He also writes the odd history book.

---------- **ABOUT THE ILLUSTRATOR** ----------

ALEX KALOMERIS is an illustrator, printmaker,
and all-around storyteller. His work revolves around creating narratives,
characters, and impressions. Nautical, natural and nostalgic themes show
up in his work and are an integral part of his identity as an artist.

---------- **ABOUT CIDER MILL PRESS** ----------

Good ideas ripen with time. From seed to harvest, Cider Mill Press brings
fine reading, information, and entertainment together between the covers
of its creatively crafted books. Our Cider Mill bears fruit twice a year,
publishing a new crop of titles each spring and fall.

CIDER MILL
PRESS

BOOK
PUBLISHERS

"Where Good Books Are Ready for Press"

Visit us on the Web at
www.cidermillpress.com
or write to us at
PO Box 454
Kennebunkport, Maine 04046